I0020121

Plainify AI

Simple for a Novice, Useful for a Pro

BY CUPID CHAN

Praise

Who knew AI and pizza had so much in common? Chapter Two uses a food analogy to explain data feeding, making it both easy to digest and fun to learn.
Aaron Poynton | Chairman, American Society for AI

Cupid Chan takes you through various learning styles with a mix of humor and insight, making even the most complicated concepts both fun and enlightening.
Tamara Nall | CEO & Founder, The Leading Niche

AI isn't just for tech experts. *Plainify AI* turns complex ideas into everyday conversations, making artificial intelligence clear and practical. Cupid Chan helps leaders understand AI's impact and how to apply it in the real world.
Bryan Howard | CEO of Peoplyst, Author of *The Vanguard Edge*

In *Plainify AI*, Cupid Chan delivers clear explanations and relatable examples that let you learn at your own pace while also offering deep insights for those who want to dig deeper into the field.
Carl Grant III | Author, *How to Live the Abundant Life*

Plainify AI: Simple for a Novice, Useful for a Pro masterfully demystifies Artificial Intelligence, transforming complex concepts into crystal-clear insights. Cupid Chan's unique approach, born from explaining AI to his own children, makes this book a revelation. Whether you're new to AI or a seasoned practitioner, Chan's accessible breakdown of machine learning, neural networks, and beyond will reshape your understanding. This isn't just another technical manual—it's an enlightening journey that makes the transformative power of AI accessible to everyone. A must-read that proves technical expertise and clarity can brilliantly coexist.
Kumar R. Parakala | USA National Best-selling author, *Lead to Disrupt*

Foreword

This book is full of "Cupidness," and let me explain why. Cupid Chan, my friend of over a decade, is a rare gem of enthusiasm and creativity, which he blends effortlessly into everything he does. Our journey together began with the "Big Data in Action" meetup in Washington, DC, in 2016. The meetup, initially a small endeavor, grew to thousands of members, a testament to Cupid's unique ability to connect people with the most complex ideas in the most approachable ways.

I still vividly remember the grand opening of our meetup at the Ronald Reagan Building in Washington, DC. While I suggested rehearsing to ensure a polished launch, Cupid proposed we take a different path—improvisation. His idea was to let the thoughts flow naturally and embrace the spontaneity of the moment. I hesitated but agreed, and the result was a lively and unscripted event filled with laughter and genuine connections. That was classic Cupid—unpredictable, yet always engaging.

As someone deeply embedded in the world of artificial intelligence, teaching graduate students and leading research teams for nearly a decade, I am no stranger to technical content. Yet, when Cupid shared the draft of this book, I found myself unable to put it down. It was more than a technical manual—it was a conversation, filled with the same humor and accessibility I've come to associate with Cupid's personality. What struck me most was his ingenious narrative structure: embedding complex AI concepts within delightful conversations with his children.

This book transforms abstract AI jargon into something anyone can grasp. It opens with a simple yet profound premise—explaining AI to children during everyday moments, from amusement park lines to kitchen experiments. By distilling technical terms like data curation, machine learning, and generative AI into relatable stories, Cupid invites readers to discover the magic of AI without intimidation. The interplay of simplicity and depth makes this book a treasure trove for both novices and seasoned professionals.

Beyond its charm, the book offers an impressive range of topics. From foundational concepts like data preparation and neural networks to cutting-edge discussions on Small Language Models (SLMs) and the ethical implications of AI, the content is comprehensive yet digestible. Cupid's explanations are enriched with vivid analogies, such as comparing data quality to pizza ingredients or neural networks to human learning—a creative touch that ensures the material resonates with readers of all backgrounds.

What sets *Plainify AI* apart is its versatility. It is equally suited for a family fireside chat as it is for a corporate workshop. This adaptability reflects Cupid's unique ability to bridge the gap between technical expertise and everyday understanding, making AI accessible and exciting.

As you embark on this journey, prepare to be enlightened and entertained. Whether you're an AI professional, a business leader, or simply someone curious about the technology shaping our world, this book promises to be an engaging companion. Just as Cupid brought life to our Big Data meetups, he brings clarity and joy to the complexities of AI in these pages.

Enjoy the ride—and maybe learn to see AI through a child's eyes. It's a perspective you won't forget.

Gordon Gao
Professor
Co-Director, Center for Digital Health and
Artificial Intelligence
(CDHAI)
Johns Hopkins Carey Business School

Copyright © 2024 Cupid Chan
Published in the United States by Leaders Press.
www.leaderspress.com

All rights reserved. No part of this book may be reproduced or
transmitted in any form or by any means, electronic or mechanical,
including photocopying, recording, or by any information storage
and retrieval system, except by a reviewer who may quote brief
passages in a review to be printed in a magazine or newspaper. The
contents of this book may not be used to train large language models
or other artificial intelligence products without written permission
from the copyright holder.

ISBN **978-1-63735-345-5** (pbk)
ISBN **978-1-63735-346-2** (hcv)
ISBN **978-1-63735-344-8** (ebook)

Library of Congress Control Number: **2024924390**

Table of Contents

Introduction

A kid's question is easy, until the unexpected one comes.

Every day, more than 70 million Hershey's Kisses Milk Chocolates are made. That means even if you keep eating one piece per minute 24/7, you still cannot finish them all in 130 years!

Besides learning this fun fact in Hershey Park, there are also many candies and rides, with which my family and I have a lot of fun. And that is also where this book was born.

Before the pandemic lockdown, when my son was 7 years old, we used to go to Hershey Park for long weekends. One famous ride, Wildcat, is also my son's favorite. While we were waiting in the long line, out of the blue, my son asked, "Dad, what are you doing at work?"

Cough cough. "Well, at work, I preprocess data before using that for training Machine Learning models or neural networks. Once the models are trained, I optimize hyperparameters and features. I often use tools like TensorFlow or PyTorch and monitor how well the models perform with metrics like accuracy and precision…"

WAIT, you wouldn't think I really said that to my son, would you? Of course, I did NOT! Not only he doesn't have the right background to understand, but also, I don't want him to think, "My dad is crazy. He sounds like speaking English, but I don't understand anything about what he said. Better not to ask him anything anymore."

So, I took a deep breath and described my daily work to him at a level he could understand. At the end of the long line, right before we hopped on the ride, he could talk back to me about what I had taught him over the past 30 minutes. This inspired me to organize our conversation, which I later shared at my AI in Action Meetup. After the presentation, my colleague Professor Gordon Gao told me, "Hey

Cupid, the way you explained AI can be useful to professionals or business leaders, too."

Oh, that's a genius idea I took to enhance the material further and present it at various international conferences. AI has grown from just a technology jargon to an everyday tool in the past few years. Even though you are unaware of it, you use it in one form or another. Like any new technology, some people are rejective because of fear and have no clue what that is. Conversely, some businesses don't want to miss and adopt the wave without accessing the risks and limitations. Both are not ideal.

As a consultant, it's my job to explain solutions to my clients so they can understand. As a professor, it's my job to teach my students so they can grasp the concept. As a father, it's my job to describe my work to my kids so they can comprehend it. As the author of this book, it's my job to simplify AI for my readers so that you can resonate with it. It is my job to **Plainify AI** – a book born from a conversation with my kids, infused with my keynotes, incorporated with my lecture, and combined with my real-life industry experience, with only one goal – explain AI in plain language, which is simple for a novice, and useful for a pro.

CHAPTER 1

Once Upon AI

Once upon a time – well, not that long ago– I found myself staring at a bag of bread. Not just any bread, mind you, but the last bag of my wife's famous Brazilian cheese bread - like the ones you can have in the Brazilian restaurant Fogo de Chão but better. As I reached for one, my kids appeared out of nowhere like a mini ninja. It's their favorite snack, especially for my daughter.

"Dad, do you think robots will ever be able to bake cheese bread as tasty as Mom's?" my son asked, his eyes fixed on the bread.

I chuckled. "Well, that's a tough one. Maybe if we teach them right."

He pondered for a moment. "But how do we teach robots as they do not go to school like me?"

And just like that, we embarked on an unexpected journey – a tale as intriguing as any bedtime story, but with algorithms and data instead of dragons and knights. I started explaining AI to him by borrowing and (over)simplifying the concept from the Turing test: "If you cannot tell an answer is from a human or a machine, then it is AI."

"Oh, is that mean if I use it to do my homework and my teacher cannot tell it's not me doing that, then that is AI?" he asked.

"Kind of…" 😄 ChatGPT was not published when he asked this question, but now it's evident that doing homework for students is one of the popular uses of AI. Whether it is ethical is another topic we will explore later in this book.

The Origin Story

A Journey Back in Time

Let's travel back to the 1950s when the idea of intelligent machines was pure science fiction. Rock 'n' roll was taking over the airwaves, and a group of scientists were dreaming up something even more revolutionary.

It all started at a summer workshop at Dartmouth College in 1956. A handful of brilliant minds, including John McCarthy, Marvin Minsky, and Claude Shannon, gathered to explore a bold idea: creating machines that could think and learn like humans. They called this idea Artificial Intelligence, a term that sounded as futuristic then as "time travel" does now.

These pioneers believed that if they could formalize aspects of human intelligence—like reasoning, problem-solving, and learning—they could program a machine to mimic these abilities. It was the birth of AI and set the stage for decades of innovation.

Key Milestones and Breakthroughs

- **The Early Programs**: In the 1960s, researchers developed programs like ELIZA, which could simulate conversation, and SHRDLU, which could understand and manipulate virtual objects. These were primitive by today's standards but groundbreaking at the time.

- **Expert Systems**: The 1970s and '80s saw the rise of expert systems designed to mimic the decision-making abilities of human specialists. They were used in fields like medicine and geology, helping diagnose illnesses and find mineral deposits.

- **AI Winters**: Progress wasn't always smooth. Funding dried up during periods known as "AI winters," when hype outpaced reality and disappointment set in. But just like any good story, these setbacks were temporary.

- **Modern Resurgence**: The late '90s and early '00s brought renewed interest in AI, fueled by increased computing power and the advent of the Internet. Landmark moments like IBM's Deep Blue defeating chess champion Garry Kasparov in 1997 signaled that AI was back and stronger than ever.

- **Deep Learning Revolution**: The 2010s witnessed the explosion of Deep Learning, a subset of Machine Learning inspired by the human brain's neural networks. Achievements like Google's AlphaGo defeating Go champion Lee Sedol in 2016 showcased AI's newfound prowess.

"Wow," my son said, eyes wide. "So, AI has been around for a long time!"

"Indeed," I replied. "It's been quite the journey, full of ups and downs – just like learning to ride your bike."

Even kids can understand

Human vs. Machine

"Let's think about what makes us intelligent," I suggested. "We can learn from experience, adapt to new situations, understand complex ideas, and use knowledge to manipulate our environment."

"Like how I learned to tie my shoes!" he exclaimed.

"Exactly! Now, machines don't learn like we do—they need data and instructions."

My readers, you may have heard a proverb:

> *"Give a man a fish, and you feed him for a day; teach a man to fish, and you feed him for a lifetime."*

At the 2017 Conference on Health IT and Analytics (CHITA), when I was asked in a panel about my perspective on AI, I borrowed this proverb with my spin:

> *"Give a computer a piece of code, and you help it solve one known problem…Teach a computer to code, and you help it solve many unseen problems." – Cupid Chan's AI Proverb*

This is how AI, or Machine Learning, to be more specific, is more intelligent than traditional programming.

AI > Machine Learning > Deep Learning

I realized it was time to tackle the alphabet soup of buzzwords.

Artificial Intelligence (AI) is the broad concept of machines' ability to carry out tasks in a way that we consider "smart." It's like an umbrella term for everything.

Machine Learning (ML) is a subset of AI. Instead of being explicitly programmed to perform a task, machines are given data and use mathematical and statistical techniques to learn and improve over time. Think of it as teaching a child through examples rather than instructions.

Deep Learning is a subset of Machine Learning inspired by the structure of the human brain. It uses neural networks with many layers (hence "deep") to analyze various aspects of data. Deep learning is particularly good at recognizing patterns, like identifying faces in photos.

"Imagine AI are the blocks in Minecraft," I said, trying to make it relatable. "Machine learning is one type of the block, say, wood. Deep learning is a special kind of wood, say oak wood."

He laughed. "I like Minecraft!"

Essential Terminologies Decoded

Data

"Data is the information we give to computers. A data set is a collection of that information. The more quality data we provide, the better the machine can practice on and learn from it."

"Like practicing piano—more practice makes me better?"

"Yes, but remember, it is a quality practice that makes you better. You will not improve if you keep watching the iPad while practicing piano."

Algorithm

"An algorithm is like a recipe," I explained. "Just like you follow steps to bake the cheese bread, computers use algorithms to perform tasks."

"So, Mom's bread recipe is an algorithm?"

"Yes, it's those steps we need to follow."

Model

"A model is an abstraction of things in real life. It's not the object itself, but you will have a pretty good idea of the actual object if you have a good model."

"That's my Hot Wheels monster truck! They look the same as the big ones we saw in the DC Capital One Arena, but they are toys and much smaller."

"You got it!"

Useful for a Pro: Some people mix **model** and **algorithm** and use these terms interchangeably. To be more precise, an **algorithm** is a set of mathematical instructions to learn data patterns. It's the "recipe" that tells the system how to learn. A **model** is the result produced by running an algorithm on data; it's the "dish" that encapsulates the learned patterns and can make predictions from new inputs. The algorithm is the learning process, and the model is the learned representation you use after the learning is complete.

Neural Networks

"These are computer systems modeled after the human brain," I continued. "They consist of layers of nodes or 'neurons' that process data."

He looked puzzled. "Our brains are in computers?"

"In a way, we've designed computers to work similarly to how our brains think. It's not a real brain, but it helps machines recognize patterns like we do."

Training and Testing

"The machine is trained by using some data set as it learns to recognize patterns there. Then we test it with new data to see how well it learned."

"So, it's like studying for a test and then taking it?"

"Spot on!"

By now, our conversation had turned our kitchen into an impromptu classroom. I could see the wheels turning in his head, which was thrilling.

Like it or not, AI is here

"Did you know we have already used AI every day?" I asked.

He raised an eyebrow. "I am?"

"Yep! For example, the app we use to check the weather uses vast amounts of data to predict the day's weather. Also, based on your viewing history, Netflix recommended *The Boss Baby* last week. These are all powered by AI."

He seemed amazed. "I had no idea AI was everywhere!"

"That's the thing," I smiled. "It's become so integrated into our lives that we often don't notice it."

Long story short, but it will continue.

"So, to answer your original question," I concluded, "could robots ever bake cheese bread as tasty as Mom's? Technically, yes. They could replicate the recipe if we teach them how to adjust for things like oven temperature and ingredient quality."

"But would they know to add extra cheese because I like them?" he challenged.

"Ah, and there's the human touch. Machines can learn patterns and preferences, but the love and intuition that goes into Mom's cheese bread—that's uniquely human."

As we put away the plate (with one final treat each), I realized that explaining AI to my son wasn't just about breaking down complex concepts. It was about sharing a story — a story of human ingenuity, curiosity, and endless possibilities when we dare to dream.

"Every great story has a beginning, middle, and end," I told him. "We're still in the early chapters of the story of AI. Who knows what amazing things we'll see in our lifetime?"

We've embarked on this journey together, starting with the origins of AI and exploring how it's woven into the fabric of our daily lives. There's much more to come—twists, turns, challenges, and triumphs.

In the chapters ahead, we'll delve deeper into the magic of Machine Learning, unlock the secrets of Deep Learning, and consider the possibilities and responsibilities of such powerful technology.

Our tale has just begun.

CHAPTER 2

Dad, I am hungry, and I want pizza. AI is hungry, too, but feed it with data!

It was a sunny Sunday afternoon. The aroma of freshly baked cheese bread from our brunch began to fade, and my kids started to get restless. My son wandered into the living room, where I was tinkering with my laptop.

"Dad, I'm hungry, and I want pizza!" he declared, his eyes hopeful.

I looked up, smiling. "Pizza, huh? Didn't we have Mom's famous cheese bread?"

"That was ages ago!" he exaggerated, flopping onto the couch. "And besides, pizza is different."

Before I could respond, my daughter chimed in, "Me too! Can we make it at home?"

I pondered for a moment. "Sure, making pizza sounds fun. But we'll need to gather all the ingredients."

As we moved to the kitchen, an idea sparked. "You know," I began, "making pizza is a lot like how AI works."

My son raised an eyebrow. "Seriously, Dad? AI again?"

I chuckled. "Did you forget what I told you in Hershey Park about what I do at work? 😄 Hear me out while we make the pizza so that both your stomach and brain will be filled.

"Ok…" he accepted reluctantly, focusing more on food for his stomach than food for thought. But I treat this as an excellent opportunity to feed nutrients to his mind.

"Just like you need ingredients to make a pizza, AI needs data to function. Data is the food that feeds AI."

My daughter thought about this and said: "So if we feed AI data, it won't be hungry anymore?"

"And the better the data, the better the AI performs—just like how fresh ingredients make a tastier pizza," I responded.

Data the ingredient

We started by laying out all the ingredients: dough, tomato sauce, cheese, pepperoni, and various veggies.

"Think of these ingredients as data," I said. "Just as we can't make pizza without them, AI can't function without data."

My daughter began arranging toppings. "So, data is important because it helps AI work?"

"Exactly. Data is the fundamental building block for AI. Without it, AI systems can't learn, make decisions, or improve over time. For instance, when you use Siri or Alexa, they rely on much data to understand and respond to your questions."

"Let me introduce you to the DIKW hierarchy," I continued, using the dough as paper to draw those letters.

"What's that stand for?" my daughter inquired.

"Data, Information, Knowledge, Wisdom," I explained. "It's a way to understand how raw data transforms into valuable insights."

- **Data** is the raw facts like individual toppings—tomatoes, cheese, pepperoni.

- **Information** is organized data, like combining toppings to make a pizza.

- **Knowledge** understands patterns and relationships. It's like knowing which toppings go well together.

- **Wisdom** applies knowledge wisely, just like I decide to make half the pizza pure cheese because I know you prefer it that way.

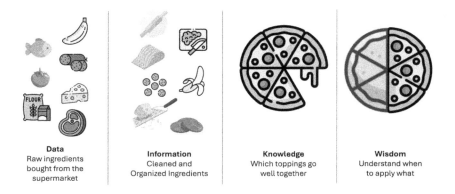

Data	Information	Knowledge	Wisdom
Raw ingredients bought from the supermarket	Cleaned and Organized Ingredients	Which toppings go well together	Understand when to apply what

Bad data, rotten tomatoes

As we rolled out the dough, I said, "Imagine if some of our ingredients were spoiled. What would happen to our pizza?"

"It would taste bad," my daughter frowned.

"Yes, and in the same way, feeding AI 'bad' data leads to poor performance. Clean, accurate data is essential."

"For example," I added, "if an AI system learns from biased or incorrect data, it might make unfair or wrong decisions."

My son nodded. "So, like using rotten tomatoes would ruin the pizza, using bad data ruins AI."

"That's a great analogy!"

Useful for a Pro: Data cleaning involves removing errors, inconsistencies, and duplicates from datasets through processes like:

- **Data Validation** checks for errors or anomalies.

- **Data Transformation** converts data into a consistent format.

- **Fill out or remove** incomplete data points if there are missing values.

It's like washing and chopping veggies or cutting out rotten parts before adding them to the pizza.

Family Meal or Personal Pizza

"Sometimes, AI systems use 'big data,' which is huge and complex datasets," I said.

"How big?" my daughter asked.

"Imagine every pizza order in the world over the last ten years—that's big data!"

"Wow!"

"Big data helps AI find patterns and trends that aren't visible in smaller datasets. For instance, companies like Amazon use big data to recommend products you might like."

"But such a big pizza is rare, right?" my son queried.

"Good observation. AI can still work with small data but requires different techniques."

"Like what?"

"For example, creating new data points by modifying existing ones is a technique called data augmentation. Or adapting pre-trained models to new, smaller datasets as in transfer learning," I explained. "It's like making a personal-sized pizza when you don't have enough ingredients for a large one. AI can still function with limited data, but it's trickier."

Less is less, More is less, but Balance is more.

"Remember when we talked about Machine Learning?" I asked.

"Yeah, teaching computers to learn from data," my daughter recalled.

"The data we feed into Machine Learning models determines how well they perform. For instance, if we're training an AI to recognize animals, we need thousands of images of each animal."

"I know! More QUALITY data is better for learning!" my son promptly responded, showing he remembered what we had discussed.

"Generally, yes. But there is a catch!

"Even if you like cheese, adding too much to this pizza will make it overwhelming and taste awful. But too little will make it plain and tasteless." I continued, "There's a balance between overfitting and underfitting."

"What's that?" my son asked, curious.

"Overfitting happens when a model learns the training data too well, including the noise and outliers, and performs poorly on new data. Conversely, underfitting is when a model is too simple and doesn't capture the underlying pattern because there is too little data to learn from, and it will perform poorly. Do you remember I taught you what's 1 + 2?" I asked my daughter.

"Yes, it's 3," she answered excitedly.

"Great, now, how about 2 + 1?" I asked her in a slightly different way.

"I don't know. You didn't teach me that," she said.

"It's 3!" My son jumped in enthusiastically and answered.

"Correct, and it's because your sister memorized the answer instead of understanding how it's calculated. She 'overfits' the math. Yet, do you remember what happened to your math quiz last week when you spent hours in the game and didn't study well?"

"Yes, I randomly checked the boxes when I didn't know the answer," he said.

"Because you didn't study enough, you 'underfit' the material and have no clue what the questions are about," I explained. "And it's shown in the bad testing scores."

My son ignored what I had just said, partially to avoid facing the embarrassing scores and partially because the kitchen was filled with a great smell of cheese!

The oven timer beeped, and we pulled out our homemade pizza. The cheese was perfectly melted, and the crust was golden brown.

"Looks delicious!" my son exclaimed.

We sat down to enjoy our creation.

"So, making this pizza taught us about feeding AI with data," I said.

"And that data quality affects how good AI works," my daughter added.

"Exactly. Our pizza turned out great because we used fresh, quality ingredients with the right balance. Ok, we had enough food for thought. Let's dive in for the food for the stomach!"

An Argument Between Two Chefs

Talking about food, there are two chefs who have opposing perspectives on cooking, and both claim their way is better. **Chef Fresh** is a superb chef who transforms his home-grown and freshly caught ingredients into delicious dishes, while **Chef Recipe** takes pride in his intricate recipes. They keep arguing about who is superior.

What do you think? Is it better with the fresh ingredient or the secret recipe?

The answer? Keep reading!

CHAPTER 3

Walk Before You Run: Shallow Learning

In our journey to understand AI, we've explored how data is the ingredient—the lifeblood—that fuels intelligent systems. Just as a chef needs quality ingredients to prepare a delicious meal, AI systems require clean, accurate data to function effectively. But data alone isn't enough. The next crucial step is understanding how machines learn from this data to make decisions or predictions.

You may recall that we briefly touched on Deep Learning. You may also have heard from somewhere else that Deep Learning is what makes AI so powerful today. Hence, you bought this book to understand more of the magic of Deep Learning. Don't worry; I will not disappoint you. You will learn that, later.

It is similar to a toddler to know how to run after mastering walking. Before we dive into the depths of Deep Learning, it's essential to grasp the fundamentals of Machine Learning. I called it "shallow learning," which refers to Machine Learning models that do not involve multiple layers of abstraction like Deep Learning models. These algorithms are simpler, faster to train, and require less computational power. They are ideal for problems with straightforward relationships between input and output. More importantly, the concepts applied in shallow learning are foundational for understanding Deep Learning, which both novices and professionals will find valuable.

Complicating simple things?

In traditional programming, we provide data and a set of rules (the program), and the computer produces an output. **Machine Learning (ML)** is a subset of Artificial Intelligence that focuses on enabling machines to learn from data without being explicitly programmed. Hence, we provide data and the desired output, and the machine figures out the rules or patterns that connect them. The pattern will then be used to get the output from the unseen inputs in the future.

These two approaches can be contrasted. For example, in traditional programming, you might write code to calculate the area of a circle given the radius with the formula . In Machine Learning, you provide a set of input data (feature), the expected output (label), and an algorithm to teach the machine how to figure out the relationship between the feature and the label itself. The machine will then find the program (model) to return the area with a given radius.

Hey Cupid, are you complicating a simple thing?

At this point, you may want to challenge "The title of this book is Plainify AI. But what you said here is to complicate a simple thing. I can easily write one line of code to calculate the area of the circle. Why bother to provide data for a machine to learn from it, which takes time, and the result may not even be accurate if I don't have enough sample data to learn from?!"

Great question! When calculating the area of a circle, ML may not be the best approach because there is already a well-known mathematical formula to describe the relationship between the radius and the area of a circle. But what if the task now is to have the machine to tell if the picture shows a dog or a cat? How can you develop the "formula" to accurately describe the features of a dog vs a cat so that that computer can follow the formula and produce a reliable result?

But if we have a lot of pre-labeled pictures with dog and cat images, we can keep providing them as examples for the computer to learn. In this case, ML is a much better way to handle the situation because there is no concrete and logical way to come up with an easy formula.

Business Casual, Vintage, or Punk. What is your Style?

Imagine stepping into a fashion boutique full of styles—from the laid-back comfort of casual wear to the timeless charm of vintage outfits, the edgy flair of punk attire, and the polished look of business suits. Each style caters to different personalities, occasions, and preferences.

Similarly, in Machine Learning, there's a style that matches every data situation and problem you aim to solve. Whether dealing with neatly labeled data ready for a "business" approach or swimming in a sea of unlabeled information that calls for a "punk" attitude, understanding these styles helps you choose the perfect fit. More importantly, these styles span across Shallow AND Deep Learning. Let's explore the fashion runway of Machine Learning algorithms and discover which style aligns with your data's personality!

Supervised Learning

When my kids started learning to speak and recognize things around them, I showed them different objects and said, for example, "This is a pen" or "This is an apple." As time passed, they recognized that a long, pointy thing was a pen and a round, red one was an apple. If they mixed up, I would show them another pen or apple again so that they kept seeing different examples until they learned what a pen and an apple are.

Similarly, in **Supervised Learning**, the model is trained on a labeled dataset, which means each training example is paired with an output label. The model aims to learn a mapping from inputs to outputs. So, the model will learn that "long" and "pointy" map to the label "pen" while "round" and "red" map to the label "apple." Depending on the types of results, there are different techniques. **Regression** predicts numerical values like housing prices, while **Classification** assigns inputs to discrete categories, such as whether an email is spam or not a spam.

Unsupervised Learning

As a science student, I learned the Law of Entropy in high school. It states that things will naturally get messier unless you put extra energy into keeping them in order. When this law applies to kids' playgrounds, it means that they will become chaos unless you put effort into organizing them. In my home, my mother-in-law takes up this responsibility.

One time, when she was back in Hong Kong taking her "annual leave," my kids' playground just became disarray. On the weekend, right before my in-law returned, my wife told my kids, "I don't care how you do it; you need to clean up your playground before grandmom comes back!"

The result? My kids organized all those blocks into a box. They call it Lego. They put those fluffy, squashy things in another box called stuffy animals. They put those little 4-wheeled things into another box called toy cars, and so on. A few hours later, without explicit instruction, they categorized the toys and put them in their not-perfect-but-decent corresponding places. That is "Unsupervised Learning."

Unsupervised Learning deals with unlabeled data. The model tries to learn the underlying structure or distribution of the data to discover patterns. Examples include **clustering**, which groups similar data points together, such as customer segmentation, and **dimensionality reduction**, which reduces the number of variables through techniques like Principal Component Analysis.

Semi-Supervised Learning

Teaching my kids often feels like walking a tightrope between giving them just enough guidance and letting them discover things on their own. I recall when my daughter wanted to learn to draw animals. I sat down with her and showed her how to sketch a simple cat and dog– these were our "labeled" examples. She learned the basic shapes and features from these guided sessions. But soon after, she began exploring on her own, drawing all sorts of creatures without any instructions– our "unlabeled" data. She started creating lions, elephants, and even mythical creatures, applying the foundational skills she learned from me to her independent drawings. Over time, her artwork became more sophisticated as she combined what she was taught with her creativity.

This blend of guided learning and self-exploration is similar to **Semi-Supervised Learning**. In this approach, a model is trained on a small amount of labeled data and a larger pool of unlabeled data. The labeled data provides the initial framework or "instruction manual," while the unlabeled data allows the model to uncover new patterns and refine its understanding independently. This is particularly useful when labeled data is scarce or expensive to obtain, but plenty of unlabeled data is available.

For instance, consider a scenario in image recognition where you have thousands of images labeled as "cat" or "dog" but millions more without labels. Using Semi-Supervised Learning, the model learns from the labeled images and then extends that learning to make sense of the unlabeled ones. This approach leverages the abundance of unlabeled data to improve the model's accuracy without the need for extensive labeling, much like how my daughter's drawing skills improved by combining my initial lessons with her experimentation.

Reinforcement Learning

Teaching kids is not always about just showing them examples in "Supervised Learning" or asking them to learn themselves in "Unsupervised Learning." Instead, we need to encourage them when they do something good. The reverse is also true: They may need to be corrected when they do something wrong to reinforce their behaviors, positively or negatively.

While less common in shallow learning, **reinforcement learning** involves an agent learning to make decisions by performing specific actions and receiving rewards or penalties, similar to how we teach a child.

CHAPTER 4

Top 10 Algorithmic Families

There are hundreds, if not thousands, of known Machine Learning algorithms. If this book aims to Plainify AI, it will be more confusing than helpful if I list them out exhaustively as a dictionary of all algorithms. Therefore, I will group them into different Algorithmic families to effectively categorize Machine Learning algorithms based on their underlying principles and structures. Each family represents a unique approach to solving a problem. Getting acquainted with the families will help you learn new algorithms even if you have never seen them before by putting them in the corresponding family.

1. Regression - Tracing Relationships and Predicting Trends

Imagine trying to predict how much money a movie will make. You might consider factors like the actors, the genre, and the director. Regression helps us find the relationship between these factors and the movie's box office success. It's like finding a magic formula, but instead of spells, we use data! At its core, regression is about uncovering and quantifying relationships between variables. By examining how these factors influence an outcome, regression allows us to make predictions, and then we fine-tune our predictions by learning from our mistakes. It's like practicing a skill – the more we practice, the better we get. Regression is a powerful tool for tasks where precision and understanding relationships are key.

Now, here's where things get a bit tricky. 'Regression' can refer to the problem we're solving – predicting how much money a movie will make (a continuous outcome). But it also refers to the tools we use to solve these problems. The two popular techniques are Linear Regression, which is the simplest form, assuming a straight-line relationship, and Logistic Regression, which predicts categories (like whether it will rain or not). Even though Logistic Regression predicts categories, it's still considered regression because it's all about finding relationships between variables. It just uses a unique trick to predict those categories. Each method has unique strengths and applications, but both exemplify the essential nature of regression: predicting outcomes by understanding relationships.

Regression

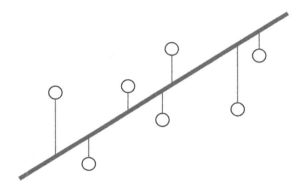

Linear Regression: Drawing the Line to Predictions

Imagine you're a gardener trying to predict how tall your sunflowers will grow based on the amount of water you give them. You notice that more water often leads to taller plants, but you're not sure exactly how much water makes the perfect sunflower height. This is where Linear Regression steps in—it's like your green thumb's secret formula!

Linear Regression is one of the most straightforward yet powerful tools in Machine Learning. It helps us understand and predict the relationship between two variables by fitting a straight line through the data points. Think of it as finding the best possible line representing how one factor influences another.

How Does It Work?

Let's get back to your garden. You record data over several weeks, noting how much water each sunflower receives and how tall it grows. Plotting this data on a graph—with water amounts on the x-axis and sunflower heights on the y-axis—you might notice that the points form an upward trend. Linear Regression helps you find the exact equation of the line that best fits this trend.

The algorithm works by calculating the line that minimizes the difference between the predicted heights and the actual heights of your sunflowers—a method known as "least squares." Think of it like this: you're trying to position a long ruler across your garden so that the total distance from each sunflower to the ruler is as small as possible. This 'best fit' ruler represents your predictive model.

Why Is It Unique and Useful?

Linear Regression is like the gardener's almanac of predictive modeling—straightforward, reliable, and incredibly useful. It's excellent for situations where you suspect a straight-line relationship between two variables. This means that if you were to plot your data on a graph, you'd expect to see the points roughly forming a line, not a curve or a random scatter. Its simplicity makes it easy to interpret; you can see how changes in one factor (like water) are expected to affect another (like plant height).

What makes linear regression unique is its balance of simplicity and effectiveness. Unlike more complex algorithms, which might require extensive computations and be challenging to interpret, linear regression provides a clear and straightforward model. You can easily see how changes in one factor are expected to affect another, making it a valuable tool for understanding and explaining relationships.

Plus, it's not just limited to gardening! You can use it to predict how a company's sales might increase with advertising spending or how fuel efficiency changes with a car's weight. And it's not limited to one input variable—you can expand it to include multiple factors, such as sunlight exposure or soil quality, to see how they collectively influence growth. This extension is known as Multiple Linear Regression.

Linear Regression offers a clear window into the relationships within your data. Uncovering these connections allows you to make informed decisions—whether you're growing sunflowers, planning a budget, or optimizing a business strategy.

Logistic Regression: Turning Odds into Outcomes

Imagine you're an event organizer trying to predict whether it will rain on the day of an outdoor concert. You consider factors like humidity, temperature, and cloud cover. Think of Logistic Regression as your weather-savvy friend who considers all those factors, crunches the numbers, and then gives you the odds of rain, like saying, "It's going to rain." This helps you decide whether to set up tents or move the event indoors.

Logistic Regression is a robust algorithm used for classification problems. Its goal is to predict discrete outcomes—such as yes or no, true or false, or even multiple categories. Unlike Linear Regression, which predicts continuous numerical values (like the exact amount of rainfall), Logistic Regression estimates the probability that a given input point belongs to a particular category.

How Does It Work?

Back to your concert planning, you gather historical weather data, noting the humidity, temperature, cloud cover, and whether it rained on similar days in the past. When you plot this data, you might notice that it's not feasible to draw a straight line separating rainy days from sunny ones because the relationship between these factors and the weather outcome isn't linear.

Logistic Regression addresses this using a mathematical function called the sigmoid function (or logistic function). This function maps any real-valued number into a value between 0 and 1, which can be interpreted as a probability.

Here's how it works step by step:

1. **Calculate the Weighted Sum:** The algorithm assigns weights to each input factor based on its influence on the outcome. For example, high humidity might be a strong indicator of rain so that it would receive a higher weight.

2. **Apply the Sigmoid Function:** The weighted sum is passed through the sigmoid function, converting it into a probability value between 0 and 1.

3. **Make a Prediction:** If the probability is above a certain threshold, commonly set to 0.5, the algorithm predicts that it will rain; if it's below, it predicts no rain.

4. **Optimize the Model:** Using historical weather data, the algorithm fine-tunes its prediction by adjusting the importance it assigns to each factor, such as humidity, temperature, etc. In other words, the algorithm learns from past weather patterns to make better predictions for your concert.

Why Is It Unique and Useful?

Logistic Regression is especially good at handling classification tasks with categorical outcomes. Its uniqueness lies in its ability to provide a classification and the probability of that classification, like your weather-savvy friend giving you the odds of rain. This probabilistic approach is valuable because it offers insight into how confident the model is about its predictions.

Moreover, Logistic Regression isn't limited to simple yes-or-no questions. Multinomial logistic regression can handle situations with more than two possible outcomes. For instance, it could predict whether the weather will be sunny, cloudy, or rainy, helping you plan for not just rain but different weather scenarios.

2. Decision Tree - Mapping the Path to Predictions

Like many children, my kids love McDonald's. Fries and burgers? Absolutely! But what they often crave even more are the toys that come with the Happy Meal.

One of their favorites was a game called "Guess Who?" where two players each select a character card and then take turns asking yes-or-no questions to deduce the opponent's character. When my kids first started playing, they randomly guessed specific characters like, "Is it the one playing the piano?" While this was fun, it often led to long games with incorrect guesses. A few days later, they changed their strategy. Instead of guessing characters outright, they began asking broader, strategic questions that eliminated multiple possibilities: "Does your character wear accessories?" or "Does your character hold something in the hand?" Suddenly, their guesses became more targeted, and the games became much shorter.

This evolution in their gameplay mirrors the fundamental principles of Decision. A Decision Tree systematically asks a series of questions that progressively narrow down the possibilities, just like my kids learned to do. Each question acts as a decision node, splitting the data into smaller subsets based on the answers. For example, in "Guess Who?", asking "Does your character wear accessories?" divides the remaining characters into two groups: those who wear accessories and those who don't. The process continues until they reach a leaf node—the final prediction or classification—which, in the game, is correctly identifying the opponent's character.

Decision Trees construct models by asking a sequence of questions about the features in your data, splitting it into branches at each decision point, much like how my kids' strategic questions guide them through the game. Each node in the tree represents a question or test on an attribute (e.g., "Does the character have blue eyes?"), and each branch represents the possible answers ("Yes" or "No"). This process continues until the tree reaches a leaf node, where the final decision is made.

Imagine a simplified visual of a Decision Tree resembling the "Guess Who?" game board:

- **Root Node**: "Does the character have glasses?"
  - **Yes**:
    - "Is the character wearing a hat?"
      - **Yes**: Possible characters...
      - **No**: Possible characters...
  - **No**:
    - "Does the character have facial hair?"
      - **Yes**: Possible characters...
      - **No**: Possible characters...

In machine learning, if you want to predict whether a customer will click on an online ad, a Decision Tree might ask questions like: "Is the customer interested in sports?", "Have they clicked on similar ads before?" and "Are they browsing on a mobile device?" Based on the answers, the tree branches down different paths, ultimately leading to a prediction of whether or not the customer will click.

The algorithm intelligently selects the questions that best separate the data into meaningful groups. It uses measures like **information gain** or **Gini impurity** to find the questions that provide the most valuable information at each step.

What makes Decision Trees particularly appealing is their simplicity and interpretability. They mimic human decision-making processes, making it easy to understand how the model arrives at a conclusion. You can visualize the decision path and see exactly which factors led to the prediction, just like my kids can recall the sequence of questions that led them to identify the correct character in "Guess Who?".

Decision Trees are also incredibly versatile. They can handle classification problems, like determining whether an email is spam or predicting if a customer will make a purchase, and regression problems, like forecasting housing prices or stock market trends. The algorithms in the Decision Tree family are often fast and accurate because they can manage complex datasets with various feature types and don't require extensive data preparation.

There are many popular Decision Trees, including Iterative Dichotomiser 3 (ID3), Chi-squared Automatic Interaction Detection (CHAID), and Decision Stump. To illustrate the algorithm, let's delve into one of the most widely used algorithms in this family: the **Classification and Regression Tree (CART)**.

Decision Tree

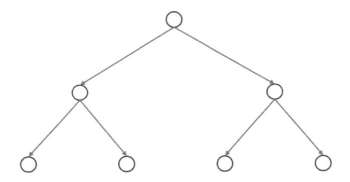

Classification and Regression Tree (CART): Carving Paths to Precise Predictions

Imagine how the judges in a cooking competition evaluate each dish. Each judge has specific criteria, like "Is the dish spicy?" "Is it vegetarian?", and "Is it plated well?" Judges follow a series of steps based on each answer to determine a final score. This is how the Classification and Regression Tree (CART) algorithm works—by systematically "judging" data at each step, it builds a precise path from question to answer.

CART is a type of Decision Tree algorithm designed to handle both classification for deciding between categories, like categorizing dishes, and regression for predicting numerical values, like predicting a dish's score. It's like a flowchart where each decision splits the data, guiding it down different paths to a final prediction, just like the judges use their criteria to arrive at a final score. In a CART tree, each split is chosen to maximize the model's accuracy—the goal is to find the questions that lead to the most accurate 'judging' of the data.

For classification problems, CART uses Gini impurity to find the questions that best separate the data into distinct categories, like separating the 'delicious' dishes from the 'okay' dishes. For regression, it minimizes mean squared error, which is like finding the line that gets as close as possible to predict the actual scores given by the judges.

How Does It Work?

You can use CART to predict whether a customer will buy a particular product. The model starts with questions that split customers into groups, making it easier to predict their buying behavior. The first question might be, "Is the customer under 30?" If yes, they go one way; if no, they go another. CART keeps asking questions like "Has the customer bought similar products?" or "Is the customer browsing during a sale?" Each question further divides the data, grouping customers by shared characteristics, leading to a more apparent prediction.

The process continues until the data is split into groups that either provide a clear decision (for classification) or give a stable prediction range (for regression). This final step, called pruning, cuts off extra branches to avoid overfitting, like a chef trimming excess leaves from herbs to enhance their flavor. This ensures the tree remains accurate and generalizable.

Why Is It Unique and Useful?

CART stands out because it can handle both categorical and continuous data, making it versatile across various applications. Unlike some other Decision Tree algorithms, which might be limited to one type of data, CART constructs paths based on actual values. This allows it to perform well with complex data, even when relationships between variables aren't straightforward.

For example, in healthcare, CART could predict the likelihood of a patient developing a particular disease based on their medical history and risk factors. It could assess the risk of a loan default in finance based on the borrower's credit score and financial history.

CART's simple structure makes it interpretable. You can easily trace each decision, see the criteria used, and understand why a particular prediction was made. This transparency makes CART highly valuable for applications where accountability is essential, such as healthcare or finance.

3. Instance-Based Algorithms: Learning by Example

Imagine you're at a massive library without a catalog system. To find a book similar to one you enjoyed before, you wander the aisles, pulling out titles that look familiar and comparing them directly to your favorite. This is how Instance-Based Algorithms operate—they don't create a generalized model upfront but instead keep the entire "library" of past data and make predictions by comparing new instances directly to stored ones.

When faced with a new problem, these algorithms search their memory of examples to find the most similar ones, using similarity measures like distance metrics. It's like finding books with similar titles, authors, or subjects in a library search. The closer the match, the more likely the new book will be similar to what you enjoyed before.

For instance, imagine you're building a system to recommend movies to users. An instance-based algorithm would store information about movies each user has liked in the past. When a user requests a recommendation, the algorithm compares their preferences to those of other users with similar tastes and recommends movies that the user has enjoyed.

These algorithms measure similarity in various ways, such as calculating the distance between data points. Think of it as measuring the distance between books in the library. Books closer together on the shelves might be more similar in content. The algorithm uses these distance metrics to find the 'nearest neighbors,' or the most similar examples, to the new instance.

Instance-based methods are sometimes called 'lazy learners' because they don't build a model up front. Instead, they wait until a new instance arrives and then find similar examples. This contrasts with 'eager learners,' which build a general model from the training data in advance.

This approach is particularly powerful when patterns in the data are too intricate to be captured by a generalized model. For example, in handwriting recognition, where each person's writing is unique, or in medical diagnosis, where subtle differences in symptoms can lead to different diagnoses. In these cases, looking at closely related examples can be more effective than trying to create a one-size-fits-all model.

Also known as memory-based learning, this family of algorithms focuses on representing stored instances and measuring their similarity. By leveraging the richness of the actual data, Instance-Based Algorithms excel at making adaptable and highly specific predictions to the context.

k-Nearest Neighbors (kNN): Predicting Through Close Connections

You're at a bustling farmers' market, looking to discover new fruits you've never tried before. You spot a fruit stand with a variety of unfamiliar options like rambutan, durian, and jackfruit. Unsure of what to pick, you decide to ask for recommendations from shoppers who have similar tastes to yours. You find a few people buying fruits you already enjoy—like apples and strawberries—and notice which new fruits they also choose. Based on their selections, you try some fruit they've picked, trusting that your similar preferences will lead you to something you'll like. This method of finding recommendations based on closely related preferences mirrors how the k-Nearest Neighbors (kNN) algorithm operates.

kNN is a fundamental instance-based learning algorithm used for both classification and regression tasks. Instead of creating a generalized model during a training phase, kNN stores all the available data and makes predictions by comparing new data points directly to the stored instances. When a new input arrives, the algorithm looks for the 'k' instances in its memory closest to the new point. It's like finding the shoppers closest to you in the farmers' market. This 'closeness' is measured using a distance metric, which calculates how far apart two data points are.

k-Nearest Neighbors (kNN)

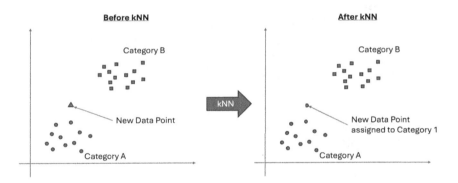

How Does It Work?

Returning to the farmers' market, let's break down the steps:

1. **Data Storage:** You remember the preferences of various shoppers, the fruits they like and the new ones they're trying. This represents the stored instances in kNN.

2. **Similarity Measurement:** When deciding which new fruit to try, you look for shoppers whose tastes align closely with yours. You assess similarity based on shared preferences for certain fruits.

3. **Identifying Neighbors:** You select the 'k' shoppers with the most similar taste profiles. If you choose k=3, you focus on the three shoppers whose fruit choices most closely match your own.

4. **Making a Prediction:** Observing the new fruits these similar shoppers are buying, say, dragon fruit, starfruit, and persimmon, you infer that you might enjoy these fruits as well. You might choose the one most frequently selected among your close matches.

In the algorithm, this process involves calculating the distance between the new data point and all stored instances to find the nearest neighbors. For classification tasks, kNN assigns the class most common among the nearest neighbors. For regression tasks, it averages the values of the nearest neighbors to predict a continuous outcome.

Why Is It Unique and Useful?

kNN's uniqueness lies in its simplicity and direct approach to prediction:

- **No Training Phase:** Unlike many other algorithms that need to be trained on a large dataset before they can make predictions, kNN doesn't require a separate training period. It's like you don't need to study a fruit guide before asking for recommendations at the market. This makes it a 'lazy learner.' This can be advantageous when the training data changes frequently.

- **Adaptability:** Since it relies on actual instances, kNN can adapt to complex data patterns without needing an explicit model.

- **Versatility:** Given an appropriate distance metric, it can handle both classification and regression problems and work with data of any dimensionality.

- **Intuitive Understanding:** Making predictions based on the closest examples is easy to grasp, making it accessible for educational purposes and initial modeling.

Therefore, kNN is particularly good at non-parametric modeling because it makes no assumptions about the underlying data distribution, which is beneficial when such assumptions are difficult to justify. By focusing on the nearest neighbors, it can capture local patterns that global models might miss.

On the other hand, kNN has some considerations: The first one is computational efficiency. Since it compares the new data point to all existing instances, it can be computationally intensive with large data-sets. Moreover, choosing the right number of neighbors ('k') is import-ant. You might get a biased suggestion if you only ask one person for a recommendation. But if you ask too many people, their preferences might be too diverse to be helpful. The algorithm must find the sweet spot for 'k' to get the best predictions. Selecting the right similarity measure is also crucial and can vary between datasets.

Support Vector Machines (SVM): Drawing the Line of Decision

I knew nothing about dancing before my daughter became a dancer. After watching more of her competition, I start recognizing different dance types. Sometimes, in a dance competition, dancers are split into groups based on their styles, for example, by either classical or contem-porary. However, suppose the stage is small and both groups' dancers are mixing. In that case, the organizer may place a long ribbon on the floor that separates the classical dancers on one side and the contem-porary dancers on the other. This ribbon tries to position to keep the groups as far apart as possible, ensuring minimal overlap. This approach mirrors how Support Vector Machines (SVM) work–they "draw" a line or boundary that best separates data points of different categories by max-imizing the distance between them.

SVM is a robust instance-based algorithm used primarily for classification tasks, though it can also handle regression. Its goal is to find the "optimal hyperplane," a boundary that divides different classes of data points with the maximum possible margin between them. In our dance example, this is like finding the perfect ribbon placement, ensuring that classical and contemporary dancers are as far apart as possible on the stage.

How Does It Work?

Let's walk through how SVM operates using our dance competition example:

1. **Identify the Margin:** SVM examines the dancers closest to the "separation ribbon" in each group. These "borderline" dancers are key because they help define the narrowest safe distance between groups, called the margin. It's like finding the dancers almost step-ping on the ribbon. They determine how wide the separation needs to be.

2. **Maximize the Margin:** The algorithm then positions the ribbon to ensure this margin is as wide as possible, keeping the groups as far apart as the space allows. By doing so, SVM creates a clear division with a large buffer zone, reducing the chance of misclassifying new dancers who might join the competition.

3. **Handle Complex Divisions:** What if the dancers aren't so neatly separable, like if they were intermingled in a circle? SVM can use a clever technique called the kernel trick. It's like lifting some dancers onto platforms and placing others in shallow pits, creating a clear separation in a 3D space even though they were mixed in the 2D floor space. This trick allows SVM to draw more complex boundaries, not just straight lines.

Support Vector Machine (SVM)

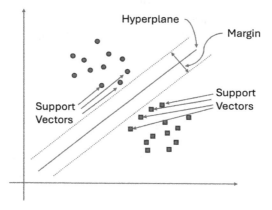

Why Is It Unique and Useful?

SVM stands out for its ability to create highly accurate boundaries, especially in cases where data points from different classes are closely packed together.

Unlike some other algorithms that might find any line to separate the data, SVM aims to find the best possible line, which maximizes the distance between the groups. It's like placing the ribbon in the dance competition not just anywhere but in the exact spot that creates the most space between the dancers. Moreover, the kernel trick allows SVM to handle non-linear boundaries, making it versatile enough to manage complex relationships in the data. SVM also performs well in datasets with many features, such as text classification, where each word could represent a dimension.

kNN VS SVM

While both SVM and kNN are instance-based, they approach problem-solving in very different ways. First, as we discussed, kNN is a lazy learner, making predictions by comparing new points to all stored instances. In contrast, SVM is an eager learner that creates a clear decision boundary (the "ribbon") during the training phase, so it doesn't need to compare each instance individually during prediction. Secondly, kNN can be computationally heavy with large datasets because it needs to compare each new dancer to all the dancers already on stage. On the other hand, SVM only needs to remember the 'borderline dancers' (the support vectors) to make a decision, making it much faster when new dancers arrive. Therefore, kNN is excellent for capturing local patterns where similar examples provide the best predictions, while SVM excels when clear, distinct boundaries exist between classes, such as in text or image classification.

4. Probabilistic Models: Solving Mysteries with the Mathematics of Chance

Imagine you're a detective piecing together a complex case. Each clue you uncover, a stray hair, a mysterious footprint, or an unusual transaction, doesn't solve the mystery outright but shifts the odds toward one suspect over another. You weigh each piece of evidence, updating your beliefs about who might be responsible as new information comes in. This is the essence of Probabilistic Models. They work like a detective's notebook, constantly updating the odds as new clues appear.

Probabilistic Models embrace uncertainty and use the principles of probability theory to make informed predictions. They consider all possible explanations and weigh them according to how probable they are given the evidence. For instance, if you're trying to predict whether an email is spam, a probabilistic model doesn't just give a yes or no. It tells you there's a 90 percent chance it's spam based on words used, sender information, and past patterns.

In medical diagnosis, a probabilistic model might consider a patient's symptoms, medical history, and test results to calculate the probability of different diseases, helping doctors make more informed decisions.

Algorithms like Naive Bayes, Bayesian Networks, and Hidden Markov Models operate by updating probabilities as new data becomes available, much like our detective revises theories with each new clue. They use a mathematical framework called Bayes' theorem to combine prior knowledge with new evidence and calculate updated probabilities.

This family's ability to handle ambiguity and incomplete data gracefully makes it unique. Unlike other algorithms that might struggle with missing information or conflicting evidence, probabilistic models can still make reasonable predictions by considering all possibilities and their associated probabilities.

This makes them particularly powerful in domains where uncertainty is a given, such as natural language processing to understand human language, speech recognition to convert spoken words to text, and predictive analytics to forecast future events based on past data. Think of how virtual assistants like Siri or Alexa understand what you say, even with background noise or different accents. That's probabilistic models at work!

By quantifying uncertainty, Probabilistic Models provide a robust framework for decision-making in the face of ambiguity. They don't just tell us what's most likely. They give us a nuanced picture of all possible outcomes, helping us make better-informed choices in everything from medical diagnoses to financial forecasting.

Naive Bayes: Calculating Chances with Simple Probabilities

Imagine you're an avid traveler who loves guessing the country of origin for postcards based on the stamps and postmarks they bear. Each stamp or postmark provides hints: a kangaroo might suggest Australia, a maple leaf could point to Canada, and cherry blossoms might indicate Japan. You use these visual clues to estimate the likelihood of a postcard coming from a particular country.

This method of making predictions based on individual, independent features mirrors how the Naive Bayes algorithm operates by calculating the probabilities of outcomes based on the presence of certain features, assuming each feature contributes independently to the final decision. It's like assuming that seeing a kangaroo on a postcard doesn't affect the chances of also seeing an English postmark.

Naive Bayes is a probabilistic algorithm that Apply Bayes' Theorem with a strong assumption that all features in the dataset are equally important and independent of one another given the outcome. Despite this "naive" assumption, which is seldom true in real-world situations, Naive Bayes classifiers perform surprisingly well, especially in high-dimensional data environments.

How Does It Work?

Let's delve into how Naive Bayes would help you guess the origin of your postcards:

1. **Collect Data:** You start by gathering information on various postcards you've received, noting the features (stamps, postmarks, languages used) and their countries of origin.

2. **Calculate Prior Probabilities:** Determine the overall probability of receiving a postcard from each country. For example, if out of 100 postcards, 50 are from Canada, 30 are from Australia, and 20 are from Japan, the prior probabilities are 50 percent, 30 percent, and 20 percent, respectively.

3. **Calculate Likelihoods:** For each feature, like a kangaroo stamp, calculate the probability of it appearing on postcards from each country. For instance, the kangaroo stamp might appear on 90 percent of Australian postcards and rarely on others.

4. **Assume Independence:** This is the "naive" part—the algorithm assumes that one feature's presence doesn't affect another's presence. So, the probability of both a kangaroo stamp and an English postmark is just the product of their individual probabilities.

5. **Apply Bayes' Theorem:** When a new postcard arrives, you use a formula called Bayes' theorem to combine your prior knowledge of how often you've seen postcards from each country with the new

evidence of the features on the postcard to calculate updated probabilities for each country. It's like combining your general knowledge of postcard origins with the specific clues on the new postcard to make a more informed guess.

6. **Make a Prediction:** You select the country with the highest posterior probability as the origin of the postcard.

Naïve Bayes Classifier

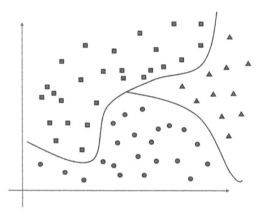

Why Is It Unique and Useful?

Naive Bayes works well even when the number of features is large, which is common in text classification problems like spam detection or sentiment analysis. It's computationally fast because it simplifies complex probability calculations into manageable multiplications. This makes it much faster than other algorithms that might need to analyze the relationships between all the features. It's like quickly recognizing key clues on the postcard instead of carefully studying every detail. Since it treats all features independently, irrelevant features have less impact on the final prediction. It also provides probabilistic confidence scores along with predictions, offering insights into how certain the model is about its decisions.

What sets Naive Bayes apart is its combination of simplicity and effectiveness despite its strong independence assumption. In many practical cases, features are not entirely independent. For example, in language, the presence of certain words often depends on others. Yet, Naive Bayes delivers accurate results, making it a reliable baseline for classification tasks.

Hidden Markov Models: Unveiling Secrets Through Observations

Suppose you're a cryptographer trying to decode a secret message that's been encrypted. You can't see the original message (the hidden states), but you can observe the coded text (the observable events). By analyzing patterns in the coded text, such as the frequency of certain symbols or the sequences in which they appear, you aim to uncover the most likely original message.

This is how Hidden Markov Models (HMMs) work. They help us make sense of systems where we can observe outputs influenced by hidden internal states, allowing us to predict those hidden states based on observable data. It's like using your knowledge of language and coding techniques to reverse-engineer the encryption process.

A Hidden Markov Model is a statistical model that represents systems with hidden states influencing observable events, especially over time. In simpler terms, it's a way to model situations where you know the outcomes but not the processes that lead to them. HMMs are particularly powerful in scenarios where the sequence of events matters, and the goal is to infer the hidden causes behind observed results.

Hidden Markov Model

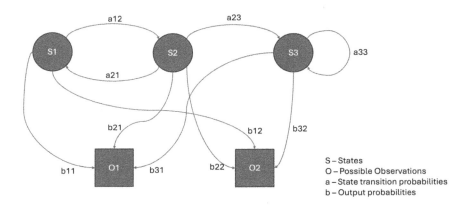

S – States
O – Possible Observations
a – State transition probabilities
b – Output probabilities

How Does It Work?

Let's dive into the steps of how an HMMs would help you decode the secret message:

1. **Define Hidden States and Observations:** Hidden States are the original letters or words of the message that you can't see. Observations are the encrypted characters or symbols you can observe.

2. **Establish Probabilities:** Transition Probability is the likelihood of transitioning from one hidden state, either a letter or word, to another. For example, in English, 'Q' is often followed by 'U'. Emission Probability is the likelihood that an observed symbol is emitted from a hidden state. That is, the likelihood a particular code symbol represents a specific letter.

3. **Sequence of Observations:** You have the entire encrypted message, a sequence of observable symbols.

4. **Apply the HMMs Algorithms:** First, use the Forward Algorithm to calculate the overall probability of seeing the encrypted message, given your knowledge of the coding system and the possible original messages. Then, use the Viterbi Algorithm to find the most likely original message by considering all possible sequences of hidden states and choosing the one with the highest probability of producing the observed encrypted text.

5. **Decoding the Message:** By applying these algorithms, you estimate the most likely original message corresponding to the encrypted one.

Why is it Unique and Useful?

HMMs excel in applications where the data is sequential and the order matters, such as speech recognition, handwriting recognition, and bioinformatics. It allows us to make inferences about hidden processes based on observable events, which is invaluable in natural language processing and computational biology. HMMs also provide a rigorous mathematical framework for modeling the probabilities of sequences, transitions, and observations.

What makes HMMs unique is their ability to handle systems where you have partial information. They account for the uncertainty and randomness in the process by using probabilities, allowing for more robust and realistic modeling of complex systems. Unlike models that treat each data point in isolation, HMMs understand that the order of events matters. It's like knowing that the letter 'Q' is more likely to be followed by 'U' in English. This ability to capture temporal dependencies makes HMMs especially powerful for sequential data. Also, it focuses on uncovering hidden patterns and structures that aren't directly observable but influence the outcomes.

Naive Bayes vs HMMs

While both HMMs and Naive Bayes are probabilistic models, they differ in key ways. Naive Bayes assumes that each clue on the postcard is independent of the others. HMMs, conversely, understand that the letters in a word or the words in a sentence are related to each other. Moreover, Naive Bayes is good at analyzing static data, like a single postcard. HMMs are designed for sequential data, like a stream of encrypted messages or a spoken sentence, where the order and timing are crucial.

5. Clustering: Unveiling Hidden Patterns in the Crowd

Picture attending a lively art festival with thousands of visitors milling about. At first glance, it seems like a chaotic sea of people. But as you look closer, you notice that small groups naturally form based on shared interests. Photographers gather near the captivating installations, food enthusiasts cluster around exotic food trucks, and music lovers converge by the live performances. Without any assigned groups or instructions, people instinctively align themselves with others with similar tastes. This self-organizing behavior mirrors how Clustering algorithms operate. Like festivalgoers finding their groups, these algorithms sift through data to identify 'clusters' of similar items.

For instance, imagine a bookstore wanting to organize its books. A clustering algorithm could group similar books together based on genre, author, or themes, even without knowing the specific categories beforehand.

Clustering is a family of Unsupervised Learning methods focused on discovering inherent groupings within data without predefined labels or categories. This differs from Supervised Learning, where you have labeled data like 'cat' or 'dog' to train a model. In clustering, the algorithm has to figure out the groupings on its own.

They aim to group data points so that those within the same cluster are more similar than those in other clusters. This similarity can be measured in various ways, such as calculating the distance between data points or comparing their features.

There are various clustering approaches, typically organized by their modeling techniques:

- **Centroid-Based Methods:** These algorithms, like K-Means, assign data points to clusters based on their proximity to central points called centroids. It's like designating meetup spots at the festival and grouping visitors by the closest one.

- **Hierarchical Methods:** These build nested clusters by either agglomerative (bottom-up) or divisive (top-down) approaches, creating a tree-like structure that shows how clusters relate at different levels of granularity. Imagine organizing festivalgoers by broad interests like art or food and then further dividing them into more specific groups like sculpture enthusiasts or vegan food lovers.

Clustering is invaluable for making sense of complex datasets by uncovering hidden structures and relationships. It's widely used in customer segmentation, which groups customers with similar buying habits; genetic research, which identifies groups of genes with similar functions; image analysis, which groups similar pixels in an image; and recommendation systems, which suggest items liked by similar users.

Let's delve into the most popular algorithm in this family to see how it transforms unordered data into meaningful groupings, shedding light on the underlying patterns that drive the data's behavior.

k-Means Clustering: Organizing Chaos into Cohesive Groups

Imagine you're a photographer returning from a trip with thousands of unsorted photos. You have pictures of stunning landscapes, captivating portraits of local people, fascinating wildlife shots, and bustling street scenes. With this overwhelming collection, you wish to organize the photos into albums based on their visual similarities. To make the sorting process effective, you decide to group the images by analyzing patterns like color schemes, shapes, and textures. This is akin to how the k-Means algorithm functions—it partitions data into distinct clusters based on inherent similarities, aiming to find central points representing each group.

k-Means is a popular and straightforward clustering algorithm that divides a dataset into k distinct, non-overlapping clusters. The "k" represents the number of clusters you aim to identify. Choosing the right value for "k" is important and often involves some experimentation and analysis of the data. The core idea is to define clusters to minimize the total distance between data points and the cluster center known as the centroid, resulting in groups with closely related members.

How Does It Work?

It begins by placing k centroids randomly within the data space. These centroids act as the initial heart of each cluster. Then, each data point is assigned to the nearest centroid based on a distance metric, typically Euclidean distance. In our photography analogy, this means assigning each photo to the closest "theme" centroid based on visual features. After all points are assigned, the algorithm recalculates the centroids by finding the mean position of all data points within each cluster. This step adjusts the cluster centers to fit the assigned members better. The assignment and update steps are repeated until the centroids no longer change significantly or a set number of iterations is reached. This iterative process fine-tunes the clusters for optimal grouping.

K-Means Clustering

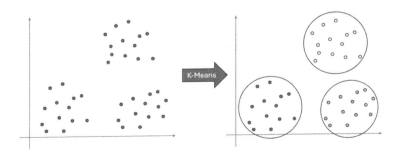

Through these steps, k-Means efficiently sorts data into clusters where internal similarities are maximized and differences between clusters are accentuated.

Consider a music streaming service that wants to create personalized playlists for its users without relying on predefined genres. Using k-Means clustering, the service can analyze various attributes of songs, such as tempo, mood, instrumentation, and rhythm, to group similar tracks together. This way, it can generate playlists tailored to individual users, like 'Morning Motivation' with upbeat songs, 'Chill Vibes' with relaxing tunes, or 'Focus Flow' with instrumental music for concentration. Clustering songs based on audio features offers users a tailored listening experience that adapts to their preferences and activities.

Why Is It Unique and Useful?

k-Means shines for several reasons: its algorithmic simplicity allows for quick implementation and execution, even on large datasets, making it ideal for applications requiring speedy results. Whether it's market segmentation, document clustering, or organizing photo libraries, k-Means adapts to various fields where grouping similar items is beneficial. Without needing labeled data, k-Means uncovers natural groupings within the data, revealing insights that might not be immediately apparent.

What sets k-Means apart is its focus on minimizing variance within clusters while maximizing variance between clusters. It seeks the most central positions to represent each group, which is particularly effective when clusters have a spherical shape in the feature space. This means that k-Means works best when the data points in each cluster are roughly the same distance from the center, like planets orbiting a star. Unlike hierarchical clustering methods that create nested clusters and can be computationally intensive, k-Means provides a flat clustering solution with a specified number of clusters, offering simplicity and scalability.

6. Dimensionality Reduction: Unveiling the Essence Amid Complexity

By now, you should know that I am a technology geek and have no sense of appreciation for art creation. Ironically, as a Washingtonian living close to D.C., I have the benefit of visiting some fantastic exhibitions at different museums. When I walk into an immense art gallery filled with thousands of paintings from every era and style, the sheer volume is overwhelming. I can't possibly appreciate each piece individually. Suppose a curator creates a unique exhibition showcasing a select few masterpieces that capture the essence of the entire collection, perhaps a vibrant Impressionist piece, a stark Cubist work, and a serene Renaissance portrait; I now gain a deeper understanding and appreciation without the overload. This is the spirit of Dimensionality Reduction.

Dimensionality Reduction techniques aim to simplify high-dimensional datasets by reducing the number of variables (features) while preserving the most essential information.

Like the curator selecting representative artworks, these methods identify the underlying structure and patterns within the data and distill them into a more manageable form. This simplification is crucial when dealing with complex datasets with dozens, hundreds, or thousands of features. These features can be challenging to visualize, interpret, or use effectively in models. The key is to reduce the number of features while retaining the essential information that captures the relationships and patterns in the data.

Consider analyzing customer data with hundreds of variables, such as age, income, purchase history, website interactions, and social media activity. Dimensionality reduction can help identify the most critical factors that influence customer behavior, such as price sensitivity or brand loyalty, making it easier to target marketing campaigns effectively.

These techniques operate unsupervised, meaning they don't rely on labeled data or predefined outcomes. Instead, they explore the inherent relationships between variables to find new, reduced representations of the data. This process can help in several ways.

First, reducing dimensions allows us to create meaningful plots and graphs, making it easier to spot trends, clusters, or outliers in the data that would be impossible to see in the original high-dimensional space. Moreover, by focusing on the most significant features, dimensionality reduction can eliminate irrelevant or redundant information, like background details in a painting, improving the performance of the models. It also enhances efficiency. Simplifying data reduces computational load, speeding up algorithms that struggle with high-dimensional inputs. It's like focusing on the key elements of the artwork instead of getting lost in every brushstroke.

Popular algorithms in this family are Principal Component Analysis (PCA), which finds the directions of greatest variance in the data, such as identifying the main themes in the art collection, and t-Distributed Stochastic Neighbor Embedding (t-SNE), which excels at visualizing high-dimensional data in a lower-dimensional map. Both serve as powerful tools for uncovering the essence of complex data. They transform the original variables into new sets of features called principal components or embeddings. They capture the most variance or preserve local relationships within the data.

By embracing dimensionality reduction, we can navigate the vast "gallery" of data more effectively, focusing on what truly matters and gaining clearer insights. It's about unveiling the essence amid complexity, allowing both novices and experts to make sense of intricate datasets more easily and confidently.

Dimensionality Reduction

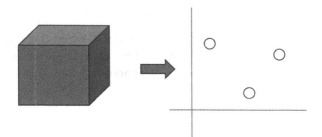

Principal Component Analysis (PCA): Distilling Complexity into Clarity

You're at a bustling international food market with hundreds of stalls, each offering a variety of exotic ingredients. The sheer number of options is overwhelming—you want to understand the essence of global cuisine without tasting every single item. To simplify, you decide to focus on the key flavors that define different culinary traditions: the spices, herbs, and core ingredients that give each cuisine its unique character.

This approach mirrors how Principal Component Analysis (PCA) operates—it reduces complex, high-dimensional data into its most significant components, capturing the essence of the information with fewer variables. It's like identifying the key flavors that define different culinary traditions: the spices, herbs, and core ingredients that give each cuisine its unique character. By identifying these fundamental elements, you gain a comprehensive understanding of the market's offerings without getting lost in the details.

PCA is a statistical technique for dimensionality reduction. It transforms a large set of correlated variables into a smaller set of uncorrelated variables called principal components. These principal components represent the directions of maximum variance in the data, effectively summarizing the most essential information while discarding noise and redundancy.

How Does It Work?

The process begins by standardizing the data to ensure that each variable contributes equally to the analysis. This step eliminates biases due to differing scales or units among variables. Then, PCA calculates a special table called a covariance matrix to see how different variables in the data are related to each other. It's like figuring out which flavors tend to go together, such as spicy and savory or sweet and sour.

By decomposing the covariance matrix, PCA obtains eigenvalues and eigenvectors. The eigenvectors, called principal components, define the directions in which the data varies the most, while the eigenvalues indicate the magnitude of this variance. Think of the eigenvectors as the main flavor profiles, like "spicy" or "sweet," and the eigenvalues as how intense those flavors are in the market. The data is then projected onto a new space defined by the top principal components with the highest eigenvalues. This step reduces the number of dimensions while retaining the most significant features of the data.

Consider a company that manufactures smartphones and wants to analyze customer preferences to design a new model. They have collected extensive data on numerous features like battery life, screen size, camera quality, storage capacity, processor speed, and more. With so many variables, identifying the key factors that influence customer satisfaction is challenging.

By applying PCA, the company can reduce the complexity of this data. The algorithm might reveal that most of the variance in customer preferences is accounted for by a few principal components—perhaps one representing overall performance by combining processor speed, RAM, and storage, another representing multimedia capabilities by combining camera quality and screen resolution, and a third representing physical attributes including size, weight, and design. Focusing on these components allows the company to tailor their new smartphone to meet the most critical customer demands without getting bogged down by less influential features, like the phone's color or the type of charging cable.

Why Is It Unique and Useful?

PCA excels in scenarios where data is abundant, but understanding is scarce. It transforms high-dimensional datasets into a lower-dimensional form without significant loss of information, making data easier to visualize and interpret. By focusing on the principal components, PCA filters out insignificant variables that may add noise or redundancy, enhancing the performance of Machine Learning models. PCA can reveal underlying patterns and relationships not immediately apparent in the original data, aiding in exploratory data analysis. It applies across various fields, from finance to genetics to image processing, and anywhere high-dimensional data poses a challenge.

What sets PCA apart is its ability to identify the directions along which the variation in the data is maximal. Unlike methods that require labeled data, PCA doesn't need any prior knowledge about the data. It's like exploring the market and discovering the key flavors on your own. By converting correlated variables into a set of values of linearly uncorrelated variables, PCA simplifies the dataset while preserving its core essence. This method is particularly powerful when dealing with multicollinearity, where variables are highly correlated and traditional statistical models struggle.

7. Association Rule Learning: Discovering Hidden Connections in the Marketplace

Imagine you're running an online bookstore, and you start noticing that customers who buy mystery novels often purchase detective board games as well. Without explicit feedback, you wonder if other such patterns are hidden within your sales data that could help boost your business. This is where Association Rule Learning steps in. It's like being a treasure hunter sifting through vast oceans of data to uncover valuable gems of insight. Imagine your bookstore data as a map; these algorithms help you find the 'X marks the spot' where hidden treasures of customer behavior lie. This family of algorithms specializes in identifying intriguing relationships and affinities between variables in large, multidimensional datasets.

For example, the algorithm might discover a rule like 'Customers who buy the latest Stephen King novel are also likely to purchase coffee and bookmarks.' This insight could lead you to create a special bundle offer or recommend these related items at checkout.

By extracting rules explaining how certain items or features co-occur, Association Rule Learning reveals important and commercially valuable associations that might go unnoticed. These algorithms use metrics like 'support,' which measures how often items appear together, and 'confidence,' which measures how likely an item will be purchased if another item is purchased, to identify strong associations. These insights can enhance product recommendations, optimize marketing strategies, and improve customer satisfaction.

Unlike Supervised Learning methods that require labeled data, such as customer reviews or ratings, association rule algorithms delve into the inherent structures of the data itself, uncovering patterns based solely on the frequency and relationships of items appearing together. It's like discovering hidden connections without any prior knowledge or guidance.

Popular algorithms in this family, such as Apriori and FP-Growth, empower organizations to transform raw data into actionable strategies, turning hidden connections into tangible opportunities for growth. These techniques are not limited to retail; they can be applied in various fields, such as healthcare, where they identify patterns in patient symptoms, finance, where they detect fraudulent transactions, and web analytics, where they understand user browsing behavior.

Association Rule

$$(A, B) \rightarrow X$$
$$(C, D) \rightarrow Y$$
$$(E, F) \rightarrow Z$$

Apriori Algorithm: Uncovering the Secret Ingredients of Frequent Combinations

Besides being a technical geek, I am also a foodie, which you may have noticed in other analogies I have given before. Let me give you one more here. Imagine you're a chef tasked with creating a new signature dish for a world-renowned restaurant. You want to create something unique and delicious, but you also want to make sure it appeals to a wide range of palates.

To craft something exceptional, you analyze thousands of recipes to discover which ingredients are most commonly used together. You notice that garlic, tomatoes, and basil frequently appear in Mediterranean dishes, while ginger, soy sauce, and garlic are common in Asian cuisine. This suggests that certain flavor profiles are inherently harmonious and appealing. This process mirrors how the Apriori algorithm operates. It sifts through vast datasets to uncover frequent item sets and extract association rules that reveal how items co-occur.

The Apriori algorithm is a foundational technique in association rule learning. It is used primarily to mine frequent itemsets and derive association rules from large transactional databases. The algorithm aims to identify items that appear together often and understand their relationships.

How Does It Work?

The algorithm starts by scanning the entire dataset to identify all items that meet a minimum support threshold, a predefined percentage indicating how often an item must appear. In our culinary analogy, this would be like noting that olive oil and garlic appear in at least 60 percent of the recipes. It then creates combinations (pairs, triplets, etc.) of these frequent items to form candidate item sets. For example, combining olive oil and garlic to see how often they appear together.

(Include a simple visual of itemsets here)

Next, we need to prune infrequent item sets. This step is crucial because it significantly reduces the number of combinations the algorithm needs to consider. It's like a chef eliminating ingredients rarely used together so they can focus on the most promising combinations. Using the Apriori principle, which states that if an item set is infrequent, all larger itemsets containing it will also be infrequent, the algorithm eliminates combinations that don't meet the minimum support threshold. The algorithm iteratively increases the size of the itemsets, repeating the candidate generation and pruning steps until no further frequent item sets are found.

Finally, it generates association rules from the frequent item sets. For example, it might say, "If a recipe contains garlic and tomatoes, there's a high chance it also contains basil." The algorithm measures the strength of these rules using metrics like confidence in how often basil is present when garlic and tomatoes are present and lift in how much more likely basil is to be present when garlic and tomatoes are present compared to random chance.

Consider a retail store aiming to boost sales through effective product placement and promotions. By applying the Apriori algorithm to transaction data, the store discovers that customers who buy diapers often purchase baby wipes and, interestingly, also tend to buy beer. This unexpected association might suggest that caregivers shopping for baby products also pick up beer, perhaps as a reward for a stressful shopping trip. Armed with this insight, the store can strategically place these items closer together, create bundled promotions, or target specific customer segments with relevant advertisements. This not only increases sales but also enhances the shopping experience by making it more convenient for customers to find what they need.

Why Is It Unique and Useful?

The Apriori algorithm excels in situations where discovering hidden patterns can lead to significant benefits. It's particularly effective in retail for understanding purchasing behaviors, enabling businesses to make data-driven decisions on product placements and promotions. The rules generated are easy to understand and interpret, making them accessible to stakeholders who may not have a technical background. Designed to handle large datasets efficiently, it remains practical even as the volume of transactions grows.

Its systematic use of the Apriori principle to reduce the search space sets the Apriori algorithm apart. By recognizing that all subsets of a frequent item set must also be frequent avoids unnecessary calculations on item sets that don't meet the minimum support threshold. This pruning process is crucial for managing computational resources effectively, especially with extensive datasets containing thousands or millions of transactions. Additionally, the algorithm's ability to reveal obvious associations and unexpected ones, like the diapers and beer example, provides valuable insights that might not surface through intuition alone.

8. Regularization Algorithms: Striking the Perfect Balance Between Simplicity and Accuracy

Suppose you're an architect designing a bridge. You could create an incredibly intricate structure with numerous supports, beams, and embellishments to ensure it stands firm. However, this complexity not only increases the cost and construction time but may also introduce unnecessary complications that could compromise the bridge's integrity under unexpected conditions. Instead, you aim for a design that uses just enough materials and supports to be robust and reliable without excess.

This principle mirrors how Regularization Algorithms function. They act as an extension to existing models, typically regression methods, by introducing a penalty for complexity. It is much like adding weight restrictions to the architect's design. This penalty discourages the model from becoming overly intricate, leading to overfitting where the model performs well on training data but poorly on new, unseen data, just as an excessively complex bridge might be vulnerable to unexpected stresses.

Consider a model predicting house prices based on features like size, location, and age. An overly complex model might memorize the exact prices of the training houses but fail to generalize to new houses. Regularization helps prevent this by favoring simpler models that capture the underlying trends in the housing market.

It achieves this by adding a regularization term to the loss function. The loss function measures how well the model fits the training data, while the regularization term penalizes complexity. This effectively balances the model's fit and complexity, like an architect balancing the strength and simplicity of a bridge design.

Regularization

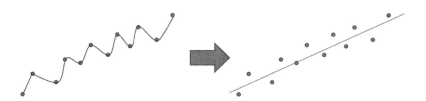

Regularization enhances generalization by favoring simpler models, ensuring that the predictive power holds when applied beyond the initial dataset. This is crucial because the ultimate goal of a Machine Learning model is to make accurate predictions on new, unseen data, not just memorize the training data.

Let's explore popular algorithms in this family, L1 and L2 regularization, to understand how they elegantly simplify models while preserving their predictive strengths.

L1- Least Absolute Shrinkage and Selection Operator (LASSO): Sculpting Models to Their Essential Form

Imagine a sculptor standing before a massive block of marble, envisioning the masterpiece hidden within. With each careful strike of the chisel, unnecessary fragments fall away, revealing the elegant statue beneath. The sculptor removes only what is unnecessary, allowing the proper form to emerge with clarity and purpose. This artistic process mirrors how the L1 Least Absolute Shrinkage and Selection Operator (LASSO) algorithm functions in Machine Learning. It methodically trims away the less important features of a model, leaving behind a simpler, more interpretable, and robust structure. Just as the sculptor carefully removes excess marble to reveal the elegant form within, LASSO eliminates unnecessary features to improve the model's clarity and performance.

LASSO is a regularization technique used primarily in regression models to prevent overfitting and enhance generalization to new data. Overfitting occurs when a model becomes too complex, capturing noise rather than the underlying pattern, which hampers its performance on unseen data. LASSO addresses this by adding a penalty term to the loss function. Think of the loss function as a measure of how well the model fits the data and the penalty term as a cost for having too many features in the model. LASSO tries to find the best balance between fitting the data well and keeping the model simple.

How Does It Work?

During the training process, LASSO adds a penalty proportional to the absolute value of the model's coefficients. This means that as the algorithm seeks to minimize the loss function, it is simultaneously discouraged from assigning large weights to any feature. The penalty term has a unique effect. It can shrink some coefficients exactly to zero.

In essence, LASSO performs automatic feature selection by eliminating irrelevant or less important variables from the model. It's akin to the sculptor chiseling away chunks that don't contribute to the final statue. By controlling the strength of the penalty through a tuning parameter, often denoted as lambda or α, LASSO balances the trade-off between achieving a good fit on the training data and maintaining a simple model that generalizes well.

Consider a real estate company aiming to develop a model to predict house prices based on numerous features: the number of bedrooms, square footage, age of the property, proximity to schools, local crime rates, architectural style, and many more. With dozens of variables, some features may have little to no impact on the price or may introduce multicollinearity, where features are highly correlated with each other, complicating the model without improving accuracy.

By applying LASSO regression, the company can identify and retain key features, such as square footage, the number of bedrooms, and proximity to good schools, while eliminating less relevant features like the color of the roof or the age of the kitchen appliances. This simplifies the model and makes it easier to understand which factors truly drive house prices.

Why Is It Unique and Useful?

LASSO's uniqueness lies in its ability to perform both regularization and feature selection simultaneously. For Automatic Feature Selection, unlike other regularization methods that simply shrink the influence of all features, LASSO can completely eliminate some features from the model by setting their coefficients to zero. It's like the sculptor deciding that certain parts of the marble are not needed at all and removing them entirely.

In situations where the number of features exceeds the number of observations, a common scenario in genetics, text analysis, or any field involving big data, LASSO helps identify the most relevant predictors, making it invaluable for dimensionality reduction. LASSO produces models that are easier to interpret and explain by focusing on a subset of significant features. This is crucial in fields where understanding the driving factors behind predictions is as important as the predictions themselves. LASSO models generalize better to new data by preventing overfitting, leading to more reliable and robust predictions.

L2 - Ridge Regression: Harmonizing the Ensemble for a Balanced Performance

Imagine you are a conductor leading a grand orchestra composed of various sections, including strings, brass, woodwinds, and percussion. Each instrument adds its unique voice to the symphony, creating a rich and full sound. However, during rehearsals, you notice that the violins overpower the cellos, and the trumpets are drowning out the flutes, causing the music to lose harmony. You can't remove any instruments because each contributes to the overall piece. Instead, you decide to adjust the volume of each section slightly, ensuring no single group dominates the performance. By fine-tuning these levels, you achieve a balanced and cohesive sound where every instrument is heard. This is akin to how L2 Ridge Regression operates. It gently shrinks the influence of predictor variables to prevent any from overwhelming the model while keeping all variables in play.

Ridge Regression is a regularization technique used to analyze multiple regression data that suffer from multicollinearity when independent variables are highly correlated. Multicollinearity can cause regression models to become unstable, leading to inflated standard errors and unreliable predictions. It's like the conductor trying to figure out which section is playing off-key when the instruments are all playing too loudly and blending together. Ridge Regression helps to disentangle these intertwined effects. It addresses this issue by adding a penalty term to the loss function. Think of the loss function as a measure of how well the model fits the data and the penalty term as a way to discourage the model from relying too much on any single variable. It's like the conductor telling the musicians, "Don't play too loud. Let's keep everything balanced."

How Does It Work?

Ridge Regression modifies the loss function during model training by adding the L2 penalty. This means the model now minimizes not only the sum of squared errors between predicted and actual values but also the sum of squared coefficients multiplied by a regularization parameter, the lambda. The regularization parameter controls the strength of the penalty. A larger lambda shrinks the coefficients more aggressively, preventing any single variable from having an undue influence on the model. This balance helps in reducing overfitting. Unlike some methods that might eliminate variables entirely, Ridge Regression keeps all predictors in the model but reduces their impact proportionally. It's like adjusting the volume knobs of each instrument in the orchestra rather than muting any section.

Consider a financial analyst tasked with predicting a company's stock price based on numerous economic indicators: interest rates, unemployment figures, consumer confidence indexes, commodity prices, etc. These indicators often move together. For instance, interest rates and inflation might be closely linked, creating multicollinearity. Standard regression could make a model overly sensitive to slight changes in the data, leading to unreliable predictions. The analyst can mitigate multicollinearity by applying Ridge Regression and building a more stable model. For example, if interest rates and inflation are highly correlated, Ridge Regression will shrink their coefficients, preventing them from undue influence on the stock price prediction.

Why Is It Unique and Useful?

Ridge Regression is particularly adept at handling situations where multicollinearity is present. It provides a solution when predictor variables are highly correlated, where traditional regression methods fail. When domain knowledge suggests that each predictor holds some significance, Ridge Regression adjusts their influence without discarding any. By penalizing large coefficients, it reduces the model's complexity, enhancing its ability to generalize.

L1 VS L2

While both Ridge Regression and LASSO are regularization techniques that add a penalty to the loss function, they differ in a few ways. Ridge Regression uses an L2 penalty, which sums the squares of the coefficients. This penalty shrinks coefficients towards zero but never exactly zero. LASSO uses an L1 penalty, summing the absolute values of the coefficients. This can shrink some coefficients exactly to zero, effectively performing variable selection. Ridge Regression retains all variables, making it suitable when all predictors are believed to contribute to the outcome. LASSO performs both regularization and variable selection, removing less important variables by shrinking their coefficients to zero. Ridge Regression is ideal when dealing with multicollinearity and when you want to keep all variables in the model. LASSO is preferable when you suspect only a subset of the variables is important and wish to simplify the model.

9. Ensemble Algorithms: Uniting Weak Learners into a Strong Collective

Imagine you're putting together a jigsaw puzzle with thousands of pieces. Each piece doesn't reveal much of the picture. Some might even seem insignificant or misleading on their own. However, when all the pieces are correctly assembled, they form a complete and vivid image that couldn't be appreciated by examining any single piece in isolation. This concept mirrors how Ensemble Algorithms function.

Ensemble methods combine multiple weaker models, often referred to as "weak learners," each trained independently, much like individual puzzle pieces. These individual models might make errors or have limitations when used alone, just as a single puzzle piece might not reveal much. But when their predictions are intelligently aggregated, be it through averaging, voting, or more complex strategies, they compensate for one another's weaknesses, like fitting puzzle pieces together to form a complete picture.

Consider a medical diagnosis system that uses ensemble methods to predict the likelihood of a disease. The ensemble might include different types of models, such as decision trees, support vector machines, and logistic regression. Each model might focus on different aspects of the patient's data, and by combining their predictions, the ensemble can achieve higher accuracy than any single model.

Much effort goes into selecting the types of weak learners to include and determining the optimal way to combine their outputs. Some popular ensemble methods include bagging, where multiple models are trained on different subsets of the data and their predictions are averaged, and boosting, where models are trained sequentially, with each model focusing on correcting the errors of the previous models.

The strength of ensemble methods lies in their diversity. By combining models that approach the problem differently, the ensemble captures a broader spectrum of patterns within the data. It's like having multiple experts with different perspectives working together to solve a problem.

Ensemble

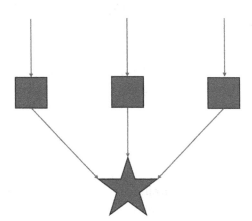

Bagging: Harnessing the Wisdom of Crowds for Robust Predictions

Imagine you're at a city fair and faced with the classic challenge of guessing the number of marbles in a large, opaque jar to win a prize. You could make a solitary guess but realize that individual estimates can be wildly inaccurate due to limited perspective. Some people might overestimate, focusing on the densely packed marbles at the bottom, while others might underestimate, not accounting for the marbles hidden in the center. Instead, you gather guesses from a large group of fairgoers, from seasoned carnival veterans to wide-eyed children, and calculate the average of their estimates. This collective average often comes surprisingly close to the actual number, a phenomenon known as the "wisdom of crowds." This concept is at the heart of Bagging, short for Bootstrap Aggregating. This ensemble learning technique enhances the accuracy and stability of Machine Learning models by combining the predictions of multiple weaker learners.

Bagging is designed to reduce the variance and prevent overfitting of complex models. Variance refers to how much the predictions of a model would change if we trained it on different datasets. Overfitting is like a student who memorizes the answers to a test instead of under-standing the concepts. They might do well on that specific test but fail on a new one. Bagging helps to create more stable and reliable models that perform well on various data, particularly those highly sensitive to fluctuations in the training data, like decision trees. The core idea is to generate multiple versions of a predictor and use them to form an aggregated predictor.

How Does It Work?

The process begins by creating multiple new training datasets from the original dataset using a technique called bootstrap sampling. This involves randomly selecting samples from the original data with replace-ment, meaning the same data point can be chosen more than once for a single new dataset.

Each of these datasets is slightly different, capturing various aspects of the underlying data distribution. For each bootstrapped dataset, an inde-pendent model (often of the same type, such as a decision tree) is trained. Because these models are trained on different datasets, they will have vari-ations in their structure and predictions. Once all models are trained, their predictions are combined to produce a final output. This Aggregating Predictions step is crucial because it combines the strengths of all the individual models. It's like taking the average of all the guesses about the marbles in the jar—the errors of individual guesses tend to cancel each other out, leading to a more accurate overall estimate. In regression tasks, this is typically done by averaging the predictions. In classification tasks, a majority vote determines the final class. This aggregation helps smooth out anomalies and errors from individual models.

Consider a medical research team developing a model to predict the likelihood of patients developing a particular disease based on factors like age, lifestyle habits, genetic markers, and environmental exposures. A single decision tree might capture certain patterns but could be overly influenced by outliers or noise in the training data, leading to inaccurate predictions.

For instance, if the training data includes a few unusually healthy individuals who smoke heavily, the decision tree might incorrectly conclude that smoking is not a significant risk factor. By applying Bagging, the research team can train multiple decision trees on different subsets of the data. The outliers might influence some of these trees, but others will not. When the predictions of all the trees are combined, the impact of the outliers is reduced, leading to a more accurate and reliable prediction.

Why Is It Unique and Useful?

Bagging stands out for its simplicity and effectiveness in enhancing model performance. By averaging the predictions of multiple models, Bagging reduces the variance associated with individual models, leading to more reliable predictions. Since the models are trained on different datasets, overfitting by individual models is less likely to impact the ensemble's overall performance. While particularly effective with high-variance models like decision trees, Bagging can be applied to any type of model to improve stability and accuracy. The independent training of models allows for parallel processing, making it computationally efficient on modern hardware.

Stacking: Layering Diverse Models for Superior Predictions

Imagine you're leading a complex international investigation involving financial fraud, cybercrime, and legal loopholes. To crack the case, you assemble a team of experts: a forensic accountant to meticulously trace financial transactions, a cybersecurity analyst to decode intricate digital footprints left across the dark web, a legal advisor with expertise in international law to navigate jurisdictional complexities, and a cultural liaison to understand the subtle nuances of the region where the crimes occurred. Each specialist provides their analysis based on their unique skills and knowledge.

As the lead investigator, you must synthesize all these perspectives into a coherent strategy to solve the case. This collaborative approach mirrors how Stacking, or Stacked Generalization, operates. It combines the strengths of multiple diverse models by layering them, using the predictions of several base learners to train a higher-level model that delivers a more accurate and robust final prediction.

Stacking is an ensemble learning technique that aims to improve predictive performance by leveraging various models and hierarchically combining them. Unlike Bagging, which uses multiple copies of the same model, Stacking brings together heterogeneous models in different types of algorithms to capture various patterns and intricacies within the data. It's like having specialists from different fields contribute their unique expertise to the investigation.

How Does It Work?

A set of different models, known as base learners or level-0 models, are trained independently on the same training dataset. These models can include decision trees, neural networks, support vector machines, and others. Each model learns to make predictions based on its unique algorithmic approach, capturing different aspects of the data. Once the base models are trained, they are used to make predictions on the training data. These predictions become new features, called meta-features, which are like clues gathered by each specialist in the investigation. These clues are then combined and analyzed to form a complete picture.

A higher-level model, known as the meta-learner or level-1 model, is then trained on these meta-features. This model learns to interpret the patterns in the base models' predictions, identifying when certain models are more accurate and how to best combine their outputs to improve overall performance. It's like the lead investigator analyzing the clues from each specialist to develop a comprehensive strategy. During the testing phase, the base models make their predictions on new, unseen data. These predictions are fed into the meta-model, producing the final prediction.

Why Is It Unique and Useful?

By combining different types of models, Stacking captures a wider array of patterns and relationships in the data, leading to improved generalization and predictive performance. The meta-model doesn't just average predictions; it learns how to best combine the base models' outputs, effectively correcting their biases and errors. There's no restriction on the types of base models used. This flexibility allows practitioners to experiment with various algorithms and select those that complement each other. In tasks where the underlying data structure is intricate and multifaceted, Stacking can integrate multiple perspectives to build a more comprehensive model.

Boosting: Transforming Weak Learners into a Mighty Ensemble

Imagine you're coaching a relay race team composed of runners with varying skill levels. The first runner, while enthusiastic, might not be the fastest, but they complete their segment and pass the baton to the next. Observing the team's performance, you notice areas where they can improve—perhaps the handoff between the first and second runner wasn't smooth, or the third runner's pacing was off, causing them to lose momentum.

Instead of overhauling the entire team, you decide to focus on each runner sequentially, providing targeted training to address their weaknesses. You work with the first runner on improving their handoff technique, then help the third runner with pacing strategies. With each practice, the team's performance improves as each member builds upon the progress of the previous one. This collaborative and iterative enhancement mirrors how Boosting works –it sequentially trains models, each one learning from the errors of its predecessor, to create a powerful ensemble that outperforms any individual model.

Boosting is an ensemble technique that aims to convert a collection of weak learners into a single strong learner. Weak learners are simple models that might not be very accurate on their own, like individual runners who might not be the fastest. But when they are combined strategically, they can form a powerful team. Unlike methods where models are trained independently (like Bagging) or combined at the end (like Stacking), Boosting trains models in sequence. Each new model focuses on correcting the mistakes made by the previous ones, allowing the ensemble to progressively improve.

How Does It Work?

The process begins by training a base model—a weak learner—on the entire dataset. This model makes predictions, but it will inevitably have errors. The algorithm then analyzes the errors made by this initial model. Data points that were wrongly predicted are identified and assigned higher weights, increasing their significance in the dataset. A new model is trained using this adjusted dataset, paying more attention to the previously misclassified data. This model seeks to correct the specific errors of its predecessor. Steps 2 and 3 are repeated multiple times. Each iteration focuses on the errors of the model before it, continually refining the ensemble's performance. Finally, all the weak learners are combined to form a strong predictor. In classification tasks, this often involves a weighted vote where models with better performance have more influence on the final prediction. It's like giving the faster runners in the relay team a longer segment to run because they contribute more to the overall speed.

Why Is It Unique and Useful?

Boosting stands out due to its sequential learning process and its focus on errors. Each model in the sequence learns from the errors of the previous one, making the ensemble progressively better at handling difficult cases. By assigning higher weights to misclassified instances, Boosting ensures that the models pay extra attention to the most challenging aspects of the data. This method often results in models with superior performance compared to individual models or ensembles that don't focus on errors. It is versatile across algorithms. While commonly used with decision trees (as in AdaBoost or Gradient Boosting), Boosting can be applied with various base learners, allowing flexibility based on the problem at hand.

10. Neural Network

How can I skip Neural Network in the Top 10? However, since it's the foundation of Deep Learning, we will dedicate the whole next chapter to this algorithmic family and explore it in more detail. As we prepare to venture into the realm of Deep Learning, remember that the principles learned here are not just steppingstones but integral components of AI. Deep learning builds upon these foundations, enabling machines to tackle even more complex tasks.

Stay curious, and let's continue this exciting journey into the depths of Artificial Intelligence!

The Verdict of the Two Chefs debate

Recall the argument between the two chefs in Chapter 2?

- **Chef Fresh:** A superb chef who transforms his homegrown fresh ingredients into delicious dishes.

- **Chef Recipe:** A chef who takes pride in his intricate recipes.

The argument between the two chefs rages on: one fiercely championing the idea that the freshest ingredients are the cornerstone of any great dish, the other passionately declaring that a masterful recipe is the true key to culinary excellence. The debate echoes through the kitchen like a symphony with clashing notes, each side sure of their supremacy. But what if the truth doesn't lie in choosing one over the other?

In the world of AI, this culinary quarrel perfectly mirrors the relationship between data and algorithms. The homegrown and freshly caught ingredients represent data, the raw facts that fuel any AI system. The intricate recipe, with its careful measurements and step-by-step instructions, symbolizes the algorithm, the method that processes the data to produce a meaningful outcome. To create a truly extraordinary dish, both the quality of the ingredients and the precision of the recipe must harmonize. The same is true for AI: neither pristine data without an effective algorithm nor a brilliant algorithm fed with poor-quality data can yield the results we desire.

Imagine one chef has the ripest tomatoes, the freshest herbs, and the finest olive oil, but no recipe to guide their preparation. The result could be a random jumble, where the potential of those ingredients is wasted. Now picture another chef with a recipe so complex and intricate that even the tiniest detail is accounted for, but their ingredients are past their prime, lacking the flavor and vitality needed to bring the dish to life. In both cases, the outcome falls short.

Similarly, in AI, clean, accurate, and relevant data is like those fresh ingredients. It's the foundation upon which everything else is built. However, data alone is not enough. Without the guidance of a well-designed algorithm, or the recipe, it cannot be transformed into actionable insights or reliable predictions. And even the most sophisticated algorithm is powerless if the data it relies on is incomplete, inconsistent, or biased.

The verdict in this debate is clear: the chefs, and by extension, AI practitioners, must collaborate. They need to marry the quality of the data with the strength of the algorithm. A dish that delights and surprises comes from the perfect union of the right ingredients and a masterful recipe. In AI, success is found at the intersection of data and algorithms, working together to create models that are as powerful as they are precise.

So, whether you're in the kitchen or training an AI model, the same rule applies: balance is key. Celebrate the data, cherish the algorithm, and remember that true excellence requires both.

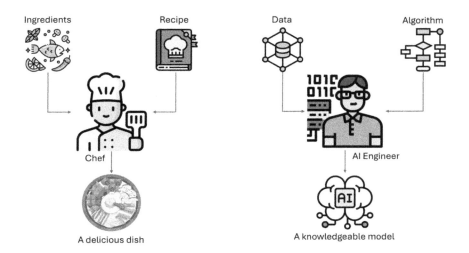

CHAPTER 5

Dive into Deep Learning Neural Networks

As we continue our journey into the fascinating world of Artificial Intelligence, it's time to dive deeper into the ocean of Machine Learning. In the previous chapters, we've walked through the fundamentals of shallow learning, algorithms that are powerful yet limited when it comes to processing complex data patterns.

Shallow learning often requires human expertise to analyze the nature of the dataset and carefully select the right algorithm to achieve optimal results. However, the rise of neural networks changes the game. By allowing models to train themselves to discern the "shape" of the data and identify the best-fitting patterns, neural networks eliminate much of this manual intervention.

Now, we stand at the threshold of a transformative era in AI: Deep Learning. This chapter will unravel the mysteries of neural networks, the backbone of Deep Learning, and explore how they have revolutionized various industries by mimicking the human brain's ability to learn from vast amounts of data.

Foundational Structure of a Neural Network

Imagine walking into a grand library where each book is a neuron, and the shelves are the connections between them. As you pull out a book (a neuron), it references other books (neurons) through citations (connections), creating a web of knowledge that spans the entire library. This intricate system mirrors how our brains work and, fascinatingly, how Artificial Neural Networks (ANNs) are designed. These networks, especially when they have many layers (hence "deep" learning), are capable of incredible things like understanding language, recognizing objects, and even creating art.

The Perceptron: The Digital Neuron's Blueprint

At the core of both the biological brain and ANNs lies the fundamental unit: the neuron. In our brains, neurons communicate through electrical impulses, sending signals across synaptic gaps. Similarly, the perceptron serves as the basic building block in ANNs, acting as a simple model of a biological neuron.

Think of a perceptron as a tiny decision-maker. It receives multiple inputs, processes them, and produces a single output. For example, suppose you're deciding whether to carry an umbrella. You consider inputs like the weather forecast, the appearance of the sky, and perhaps even a twinge in your knee predicting rain. Weighing these factors, you make a decision. This is essentially how a perceptron operates.

Mathematically, a perceptron takes input values, multiplies each by a corresponding weight, sums them up, adds a bias, and then passes the result through an activation function to produce an output. This activation function is like a switch that introduces non-linearity, allowing the network to learn more complex patterns than a simple straight line. A common example is the sigmoid function, which squashes the output between 0 and 1. This process allows the perceptron to model complex decision boundaries and make informed decisions based on the input data.

Perceptron

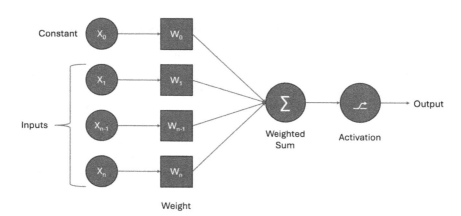

Weights and Biases: Tuning the Network's Sensitivity

Weights and biases are the secret sauce that gives neural networks their learning capability. Weights are like volume knobs controlling the influence of each input on the neuron's output. If you're mixing a song, you might increase the volume of the vocals while decreasing the drums to achieve the perfect balance. Similarly, in a neural network, adjusting the weights amplifies or diminishes the importance of each input.

For instance, in facial recognition, certain pixels, as inputs, might be more crucial in identifying features like eyes or the shape of the mouth. By assigning higher weights to these pixels, the network pays more attention to them during processing.

Biases act as a baseline adjustment, much like setting the thermostat in your house. Regardless of the inputs of outside temperature, the thermostat as bias ensures your home stays at a comfortable level. In neural networks, the bias allows the activation function to be shifted left or right, providing flexibility in how the neuron activates. It ensures that neurons can fire even if the weighted sum of inputs is zero, adding an extra degree of freedom to the model.

Bringing It All Together: Processing Inputs to Outputs

Consider a simple scenario: you're trying to determine if an email is spam. The perceptron receives inputs like the presence of certain keywords, the sender's address, and the email's formatting. Each of these inputs is weighted according to its significance in identifying spam.

Weights amplify inputs that are strong indicators of spam (like suspicious keywords) and downplay less relevant factors. Bias adjusts the neuron's tendency to label emails as spam or not, based on the overall distribution of your inbox. The perceptron processes these weighted inputs, sums them up with the bias, and then applies an activation function (like the sigmoid function) to produce the output: spam or not spam.

The Network Effect: Neurons Working in Harmony

While a single perceptron can make basic decisions, the true power of ANNs comes from linking multiple perceptrons together across layers. This interconnectedness allows the network to learn and represent complex patterns, much like our brains do. This is where the "deep" in Deep Learning comes in. These networks have multiple "hidden" layers between the input and output, allowing them to extract intricate features and relationships from the data.

Input Layer receives the initial data (like pixel values of an image). **Hidden Layers** process inputs through multiple perceptrons, allowing the network to learn intricate features (like edges, shapes, and textures in images). This is where the magic of Deep Learning happens, as the network learns to represent the data in increasingly abstract and meaningful ways. **Output Layer** produces the final prediction or classification (like identifying the image as a cat or a dog). Each connection between neurons in these layers has its own weight and bias, all of which are adjusted during the training process. This adjustment is done through algorithms like backpropagation, which fine-tune the weights and biases to minimize errors in the network's predictions.

The Biological Parallel: Learning from the Brain

Our brains strengthen or weaken synaptic connections based on experiences; a concept known as synaptic plasticity. Similarly, ANNs adjust weights and biases through learning algorithms, improving their performance over time.

For example, when learning to ride a bike, your brain reinforces the neural pathways that help you balance and pedal simultaneously. In ANNs, training on more data helps the network adjust its parameters to better recognize patterns, much like practice improves our skills. This ability to learn from data is what makes Deep Learning so powerful and applicable to a wide range of problems.

The Foundation for Intelligence

Understanding perceptrons, weights, and biases gives us a window into how neural networks mimic cognitive functions. They transform raw data into meaningful insights by adjusting connections and thresholds, much like our brains process sensory information to make decisions.

Whether you're just starting your journey into AI or refining your expertise, appreciating this foundational structure is crucial. It's the bedrock upon which more complex architectures and algorithms are built, enabling advancements in fields like computer vision, natural language processing, and beyond. For example, these concepts are essential for understanding how self-driving cars perceive their surroundings, how virtual assistants understand our commands, and how medical imaging systems detect diseases.

As we continue to explore deeper layers and more sophisticated models, remember that it all starts with the humble perceptron, our digital neuron, and the elegant interplay of weights and biases that bring Artificial Intelligence to life.

Activation and Transformation: Breathing Life into Neurons

Imagine you're at a concert, and the atmosphere is electric. The musicians are poised, instruments ready, but the show doesn't truly begin until the first note resonates through the air. That initial sound ignites the crowd, transforming the setting from a silent stage to a vibrant experience. In the realm of neural networks, the activation function plays a similar role. It decides when a neuron should "sing" or remain silent, bringing the network to life.

The Neuron's Decision Maker

In our previous exploration, we discussed how neurons receive inputs, weigh them, and sum them up with a bias. However, this raw total isn't very useful on its own. Enter the activation function, the neuron's decision-making process that transforms this total input into an output signal.

Think of the activation function as a gatekeeper. It evaluates the neuron's aggregated input and determines whether it should activate. This is to fire or not. This process introduces non-linearity into the network, enabling it to learn and model complex patterns that linear functions simply can't capture.

Why Non-Linearity Matters

Consider trying to separate apples from oranges using a straight line on a graph where fruits are plotted based on features like weight and color. If the fruits are mixed in such a way that a straight line can't separate them, you need a more flexible approach—a curve or multiple lines.

Similarly, neural networks need non-linear activation functions to handle data that isn't linearly separable.

Without activation functions introducing non-linearity, no matter how many layers our network has, it would essentially behave like a single-layer network. It would be limited to modeling linear relationships, severely restricting its problem-solving capabilities.

Common Activation Functions: The Cast of Characters

Activation functions allow neural networks to learn complex representations by enabling neurons to respond to various patterns in the data. They help the network to capture non-linear relationships, which are abundant in real-world data.

For example, in image recognition, edges, textures, and shapes are not linearly related to pixel values. Activation functions allow neurons in hidden layers to detect these features by responding differently to various input patterns. Let's delve into some of the most widely used activation functions, each adding its own flavor to how neurons process information.

Sigmoid Function

The sigmoid function squashes input values into a range between 0 and 1. It's like a dimmer switch for a light—you can adjust the brightness smoothly from off (0) to fully on (1).

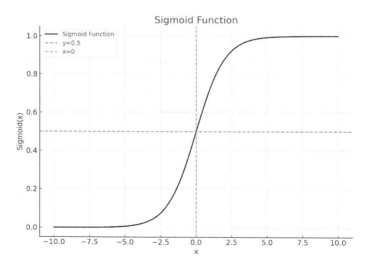

This function maps any input value to a value between 0 and 1, which can be interpreted as a probability. This makes it particularly useful in the output layer for binary classification problems, where we want to predict the likelihood of an event.

Hyperbolic Tangent (tanh)

The hyperbolic tangent is similar to the sigmoid, but it ranges between -1 and 1. It's like a thermostat that can adjust temperature both above and below a baseline.

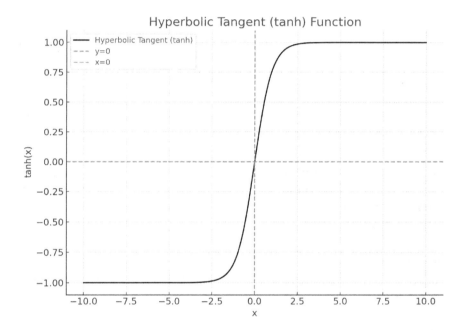

The tanh function centers the outputs around zero, which can sometimes make learning in certain networks more efficient.

Rectified Linear Unit (ReLU)

ReLU is the workhorse of modern neural networks. It outputs zero if the input is negative and outputs the input itself if it's positive.

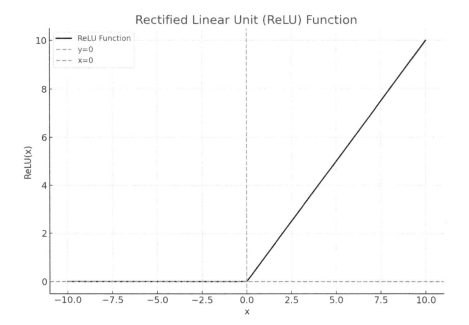

Imagine a one-way valve that only allows water to flow through if there's positive pressure. ReLU introduces non-linearity while being computationally efficient. It's often the preferred choice for hidden layers in Deep Learning models.

Variations of ReLU, like Leaky ReLU and Parametric ReLU, address some of its limitations by allowing a small, non-zero gradient for negative inputs, which can sometimes improve training.

Softmax Function

Used primarily in the output layer for multi-class classification, softmax converts raw scores into probabilities that sum up to 1.

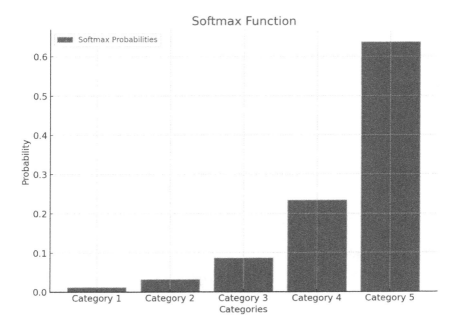

It's like divvying up a pie among friends—each person gets a slice proportional to their appetite. Softmax ensures that the outputs represent a probability distribution across multiple classes.

Choosing the Right Activation Function

Selecting an appropriate activation function is crucial and often depends on the problem at hand. Sigmoid and tanh are useful for models where outputs need to be bounded between a certain range. ReLU is generally a good starting point for hidden layers in Deep Learning models due to its simplicity and efficiency. Softmax is ideal for classification tasks where outputs represent probabilities across multiple classes.

The choice affects not only the performance but also the training dynamics of the network. For instance, sigmoid and tanh can suffer from vanishing gradient problems in deep networks, making training difficult. ReLU mitigates this issue, allowing for faster and more effective learning. Hence, each activation function has a different purpose to fit for different scenario.

The Learning Journey: From Inputs to Insights

Activation functions are also essential for the backpropagation process, where the network learns from errors by adjusting weights and biases. During training, the **Forward Pass** is the process of which inputs are transformed into outputs through weighted sums and activation functions. Then **Error Calculation** computes the difference between the predicted output and the actual output.

In the **Backward Pass**, the error is propagated back through the network, and gradients are calculated using derivatives of activation functions. This is then followed by **Parameter Update** in which weights and biases are adjusted to minimize the error. Activation functions must be differentiable to facilitate this learning process. Their derivatives influence how quickly and effectively the network converges to an optimal solution.

Information Flow: Navigating Data Through the Network

Visualize you're navigating a maze to find the treasure at its center. Each twist and turn represents a decision, and every corridor you choose brings you closer to, or farther from, your goal. In a neural network, this journey mirrors the movement of data through layers of interconnected neurons, a process known as Forward Propagation. But how do we know if we're on the right path? That's where the Loss Function acts as our guide, like a compass pointing out how far we are from the treasure. It evaluates our current position and helps us recalibrate our direction, ensuring we adjust course and get closer to the ultimate goal.

Forward Propagation: The Data's Expedition Through Layers

Forward propagation is the mechanism by which input data travels through the neural network to generate an output. Think of it as a relay race where each runner (neuron) passes the baton (data) to the next runner, collectively working towards the finish line (final output). Let's refresh what we learnt by chaining them into the Forward Propagation process.

Input Layer: The race begins with the input layer receiving raw data. This could be numerical values, images, or text—anything that can be converted into a numerical format the network understands.

Hidden Layers: The data then moves through one or more hidden layers. In each neuron within these layers, the input data is multiplied by weights and summed up with biases, reflecting the neuron's current parameters. This sum is transformed using an activation function, determining whether the neuron should activate and pass the signal forward.

Output to Next Layer: The activated output becomes input for the neurons in the subsequent layer.

Output Layer: The final layer aggregates the processed data to produce the network's output, be it a prediction, classification, or decision.

Loss Function: Gauging Prediction Accuracy

You now got your result from the Output Layer, and you WISH that is correct. But you should KNOW this will not happen in the first shot. Just like when you're shooting arrows at a target, each shot lands somewhere on the board. But without measuring the distance from the bullseye, you can't tell how to adjust your aim. The Loss Function in a neural network serves as this measurement. It quantifies the difference between the predicted outputs and the actual targets.

It acts as a Performance Indicator to provide a numerical value representing how well the network is performing on a given task. By calculating the loss, we can determine how to adjust the network's parameters to reduce errors in future predictions as a guidance for improvement. Common loss functions include:

Mean Squared Error (MSE): Used for regression problems where the goal is to predict continuous values. It calculates the average squared difference between the predicted and actual values.

Cross-Entropy Loss: Ideal for classification tasks, measuring the difference between two probability distributions, the predicted probabilities and the actual labels.

Hinge Loss: Often used in support vector machines for binary classification tasks. It penalizes misclassifications linearly.

Mean Absolute Error (MAE): It calculates the average absolute difference between predicted and actual values.

The Synergy of Forward Propagation and Loss Function

Think of forward propagation and the loss function like cooking a new dish following a recipe. You start with raw ingredients, the Input, with vegetables, spices, proteins. Throughout the cooking process, the Forward Propagation, you process these ingredients according to the recipe steps such as chopping, mixing, and heating.

Each step transforms the ingredients, much like data is transformed as it moves through the network's layers. In the taste test is the Loss Function, of which you and your friends taste the dish to see how close it is to the desired flavor. If it's too salty or lacks spice, this feedback helps you understand what adjustments are needed. Based on the taste test, you might add more seasoning or adjust the cooking time, aiming to improve the final dish. This is the optimization, where the goal is to adjust the network's parameters to minimize the loss.

Setting the Stage for Optimization

The loss function doesn't just tell us that there's an error; it provides a roadmap for reducing it. This is critical for the optimization process, where the goal is to adjust the network's parameters to minimize the loss.

By computing the gradient of the loss function with respect to each weight and bias, we understand how a small change in these parameters affects the loss. This gradient points in the direction of the steepest increase in the loss function. Then, we use optimization algorithms like gradient descent to adjust the weights and biases in the opposite direction of the gradient, which decreases the loss. This process repeats over many iterations, gradually improving the network's performance.

Imagine standing at the top of a hill (representing high loss) and wanting to reach the valley below (representing low loss). The landscape is uneven, and you can't see very far ahead. By feeling the slope under your feet (calculating the gradient), you decide which direction to take a step to descend.

So, **Forward Propagation** determines your current position on the hill by processing inputs to produce an output and calculating the loss. Then the **Loss Function** measures how high up the hill you are. The higher the loss, the further you are from your goal. By **Gradient Calculation**, you feel the slope of the hill, indicating the steepest descent direction. **Updating Parameter** happens when you take a step downhill, adjusting weights and biases to reduce the loss. By continually repeating this process, you navigate towards the valley, minimizing the loss and improving the network's predictions.

Learning is a Process: Optimizing the Network's Performance

When you're tuning a musical instrument, with each adjustment of the strings or keys, you refine the sound, striving for harmony and resonance. Similarly, in neural networks, the optimization process fine-tunes the model's parameters, its weights and biases, to achieve peak performance. This meticulous calibration is carried out through a symphony of techniques like Backward Propagation, Gradient Descent, and the precise adjustment of the Learning Rate, ensuring the model hits all the right notes in its predictions.

Backward Propagation: Learning from Errors

After forward propagation computes the output and the loss function measures the error, the question arises: How do we adjust the network's parameters to reduce this error? Backward Propagation, or backpropagation, is the method that answers this question. It's akin to retracing your steps after getting lost, identifying where you took a wrong turn to avoid making the same mistake again.

The process starts at the output layer, where the error between the predicted and actual outputs is calculated and how the error forward propagates through the network.

The error is then propagated backward through the network layers. At each neuron, we compute the gradient of the loss function with respect to the weights and biases. This involves calculating partial derivatives, which tell us how a small change in a weight or bias affects the overall loss.

Using these gradients, we adjust the weights and biases in the opposite direction of the gradient, since we want to minimize the loss. This is like noticing that stepping east led you away from your destination, so you decide to step west instead.

Backpropagation ensures that each neuron in the network learns how it contributed to the error, allowing for precise adjustments. It distributes the responsibility of error correction throughout the network, much like a team working together to solve a problem by addressing individual contributions.

Gradient Descent: Navigating the Error Landscape

To effectively update the network's parameters, we need a strategy for moving towards the minimum of the loss function of the point where the error is smallest. Gradient Descent is the algorithm that facilitates this journey. Think of it as hiking down a mountain in foggy conditions; you can't see the entire path, but by feeling the slope underfoot, you can determine the direction that leads downhill.

At your current position with the current set of weights and biases, you calculate the gradient of the loss function. The gradient is a vector that points in the direction of the steepest ascent. Imagine it as a ball rolling down a hill; the gradient tells you the direction the ball would roll.

To decrease the loss, you move in the opposite direction of the gradient. That is the direction of the steepest descent.

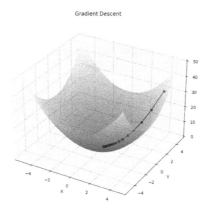

The weights and biases are updated by taking the current parameter values and subtract a small portion of the gradient. This ensures that we move the parameters in the direction that reduces the loss.

This process is repeated iteratively, with each update ideally bringing the network closer to the point where the loss is minimized. There are a few common variations of Gradient Descent. For example, **Batch Gradient Descent** uses the entire training dataset to compute the gradient. While accurate, it's computationally intensive for large datasets. **Stochastic Gradient Descent (SGD)** updates parameters using one training example at a time. This introduces noise into the updates but allows for faster iterations and can help escape local minima. **Mini-Batch Gradient Descent** strikes a balance by updating parameters using small batches of training data. It's widely used in practice due to its efficiency and performance benefits. Each variation has its trade-offs, and the choice often depends on the specific problem and dataset size.

The Learning Rate: Balancing the Steps

The Learning Rate is a crucial hyperparameter in the optimization process. It determines the size of the steps we take in the parameter space during gradient descent. Imagine trying to find your way down a mountain, taking too large a step with high learning rate means you risk overshooting the valley or missing the path entirely, much like leaping without looking. On the other hand, taking too small a step with low learning rate means the progress becomes painfully slow, and it may take an impractical amount of time to reach the bottom, akin to inching forward timidly.

So, finding the right balance is essential. A properly set learning rate ensures that each update moves the parameters closer to the loss minimum without overshooting as a controlled descent. It's also worth noting that we need to set the learning rate before the training starts. We call this kind of setting Hyperparameters and will explore it more later in this chapter.

The Challenges of Optimization

The loss landscape can have many local minima (valleys) and saddle points (flat regions) where gradients are near zero, potentially trapping the optimization process. Imagine getting stuck in a small valley on the mountain; it seems like the lowest point, but there might be a deeper valley elsewhere. This phenomenon is called local minima and saddle points.

Besides, the network might learn the training data too well, capturing noise instead of underlying patterns, leading to poor generalization of new data. This overfitting is like memorizing the answers to a test instead of understanding the concepts; you might do well on that specific test, but you won't be able to apply the knowledge to new problems.

Moreover, large networks with millions of parameters require significant computational resources for optimization, which is highly computationally complex.

Several techniques can address these challenges. For example, as we saw earlier in this book, **Regularization Techniques** like dropout or L2 regularization can prevent overfitting by adding constraints to the optimization process. **Advanced Optimization Algorithms** like Adam combine momentum and adaptive learning rates to navigate complex loss landscapes more effectively. Finally, we can also tune **Hyperparameters** to systematically adjust learning rates, batch sizes, and network architectures to find the optimal configuration.

Hyperparameters: Tuning the Neural Network's Performance

In an orchestra, each musician contributes to the overall success of the performance. To create a harmonious symphony, a conductor must make critical decisions: how fast should the tempo be? How many rehearsals are needed? How large should each section of the orchestra be? Similarly, when training a neural network, you must set hyperparameters, the adjustable settings that govern the learning process. These parameters aren't learned from the data but are defined before training begins, significantly influencing the model's performance.

Hyperparameters are the knobs and dials that you, as the model designer, can tweak to control the learning process of a neural network. They differ from parameters like weights and biases, which the network learns during training. Hyperparameters must be set before training and can profoundly affect the network's ability to learn from data.

In neural networks, improper hyperparameter settings can lead to underfitting of which the model is too simple to capture the underlying patterns, or overfitting of which the model is too complex and captures noise rather than the signal.

Learning Rate: Controlling the Pace of Learning

Remember that in the last section, we discussed the one arguably the most critical hyperparameter, the Learning Rate. It determines the size of the steps the optimization algorithm takes when updating the network's weights and biases during training.

A high learning rate allows the model to learn quickly but risks over-shooting the optimal parameters, potentially missing the minimum of the loss function. Conversely, a low learning rate ensures more precise convergence but can slow the training process. If the learning rate is too high, the model's parameters might oscillate or diverge, causing the learning process to fail.

Think of learning to play a musical instrument. If you practice too quickly (high learning rate), you might make many mistakes and fail to improve. If you practice too slowly (low learning rate), progress will be minimal, and you might lose motivation.

You may ask, "So, what's the best way to pick the Learning Rate?" There are a few common ways: first, by experimentation. You can start with standard values (e.g., 0.01 or 0.001) and adjust based on the model's performance. Another common way is to reduce the learning rate over time to allow for finer adjustments as training progresses. For more advanced approaches, we can use adaptive learning rates with optimization algorithms like Adam or RMSProp that adjust the learning rate dynamically for each parameter.

A well-chosen learning rate can accelerate convergence and improve the model's accuracy. It ensures that the optimization process moves steadily towards the loss minimum without overshooting or getting stuck.

Epochs: The Number of Training Cycles

An Epoch represents one complete pass through the entire training dataset. It defines how many times the learning algorithm will work through the whole dataset.

Multiple epochs allow the model to learn from the data repeatedly, improving its ability to generalize from the examples. Too few epochs might lead to underfitting, where the model hasn't learned enough from the data. Too many epochs can cause overfitting, where the model learns noise and irrelevant details.

Consider studying for an exam. Reading your notes once (one epoch) might not be enough to grasp the material thoroughly. Repeatedly reviewing them helps reinforce your understanding. However, over-studying can lead to diminishing returns or even confusion.

Therefore, it is crucial to monitor performance using validation data after each epoch. Training should stop when the validation loss stops improving. We can also implement techniques that halt training when no significant improvement is observed, preventing overfitting. Choosing the right number of epochs ensures that the model has adequately learned from the data without wasting computational resources or overfitting.

Batch Size: The Number of Samples Per Update

The Batch Size determines how many training examples are used to calculate the gradient and update the model's parameters in one iteration. Larger batch sizes require more memory, as more data must be loaded into memory at once. Smaller batch sizes introduce more noise into the training process due to higher variance in the gradient estimates, which can help the model escape local minima but might also slow down convergence.

Imagine filling a swimming pool using buckets (iterations). A large bucket (large batch size) fills the pool faster but requires more strength (memory). A small bucket (small batch size) is easier to handle but requires more trips (iterations) to fill the pool.

Batch size is often determined by hardware constraints, such as the hardware's available memory (e.g., GPU, and memory). Due to computational efficiency, common batch sizes can be set by empirical testing using powers of two (e.g., 32, 64, 128). A moderate batch size (neither too small nor too large) often balances convergence speed and stability.

Batch size affects the speed and stability of the training process. It influences how quickly the model learns and how noisy the updates are, impacting the overall convergence.

Number of Layers: Defining the Network's Depth

The Number of Layers refers to the depth of the neural network. It defines the count of hidden layers between the input and output layers. More layers enable the network to learn more complex representations and capture intricate patterns in the data. Deeper networks provide higher model capacity but require more computational resources and may take longer to train. However, very deep networks can suffer from issues where gradients become too small or too large, hindering training.

Think of layers as filters in a water purification system. Each additional filter removes more impurities, resulting in cleaner water. However, too many filters might slow down the flow or be redundant. So, we should start simple. Begin with a shallow network and gradually add layers to see if performance improves.

We should also consider the problem's complexity. Complex tasks like image recognition or natural language processing often benefit from deeper networks. Many people have done research that has proven effective for specific tasks. Don't reinvent the wheel but use those established architectures if they match your needs. We will see some of those invented wheels in the next chapter.

The number of layers affects the network's ability to model complex functions. A network that's too shallow might not capture the necessary patterns, while one that's too deep might overfit or be challenging to train effectively.

The Art of Hyperparameter Tuning

Hyperparameters are the essential settings that you, as the model architect, must carefully choose to guide the neural network's learning process. They are the levers that control the model's pace, capacity, and behavior during training.

- **Learning Rate**: Dictates how quickly the model learns and its balancing speed and accuracy.

- **Epochs**: Determines how many times the model sees the training data, affecting its ability to generalize.

- **Batch Size**: Influences the stability and efficiency of training through gradient updates.

- **Number of Layers**: Sets the depth of the network, controlling its capacity to model complex patterns.

Finding the optimal hyperparameters is often an iterative process involving experimentation, validation, and experience. It's a blend of science and art, requiring a deep understanding of both the underlying algorithms and the problem domain.

By thoughtfully tuning these hyperparameters, you empower your neural network to learn effectively, striking the right balance between underfitting and overfitting, and ultimately achieving better performance on unseen data.

You are the best!

Imagine attending a global talent showcase where various performers demonstrate their unique skills. Some excel at juggling ten balls at once, others at performing standup comedy, and a few at singing and dancing like those K-pop stars. Amidst them stands a performer who not only masters each of these skills but also blends them seamlessly into a captivating act. In the realm of Machine Learning, neural networks often take on this star role. They have risen to prominence due to their remarkable ability to tackle a wide array of complex tasks with exceptional proficiency.

One of the attributes of neural networks that make them very compelling is their versatility. They are like Swiss Army knives in the Machine Learning toolbox, adept at handling diverse types of data and tasks. Neural networks, particularly deep ones, have the theoretical capability to approximate any continuous function. This means they can model highly complex relationships that other algorithms might struggle to capture. Think of it as if the relationship between your data and the desired output is a complex curve. A neural network can learn to fit that curve much better than a simpler model like a straight line.

Unlike traditional models that require manual feature engineering, neural networks can automatically learn hierarchical representations from raw data. For example, in image recognition, they can autonomously detect edges, textures, and shapes without explicit programming. This is like having a chef who can not only cook delicious dishes but also source the ingredients themselves.

From computer vision and natural language processing to speech recognition and gameplay, neural networks have made significant strides in multiple fields, often outperforming specialized algorithms. They've proven their worth in diverse areas, such as predicting stock prices, translating languages, and even composing music.

By stacking multiple layers of neurons, they can capture intricate patterns through successive transformations. Each layer learns to represent data at a different level of abstraction. Imagine each layer as a different level of understanding; the deeper you go, the more nuanced the network's comprehension becomes.

Activation functions introduce non-linearity, enabling the network to model phenomena where the relationship between inputs and outputs isn't straightforward. This is crucial for capturing the complexity of real-world data, where things aren't always as simple as a cause-and-effect relationship.

Neural networks can process data with many features, effectively managing the "curse of dimensionality" that hampers other algorithms. For example, they can analyze images with millions of pixels or text documents with thousands of words without getting overwhelmed.

While no single model is universally superior for every task, neural networks have proven to be exceptionally effective across many challenging problems. Their ability to learn from data in ways that mirror human cognition allows them to tackle tasks that were once considered the exclusive domain of human intelligence.

As we stand on the shoulders of this technological marvel, it's clear why neural networks are often hailed as the pinnacle of Machine Learning models. They embody the fusion of mathematical rigor, computational power, and the ingenuity to mimic complex patterns in data, earning them the title of "the best" in many eyes. But after reading this whole chapter, you start feeling hungry and notice that it's dinner time…

Grandma recipe vs three-star Michelin Restaurant

...it's dinner time and you are deciding where to go. On one side is a three-star Michelin restaurant, offering culinary artistry with intricate flavors and an unmatched ambiance. On the other is your grandma's house, where the comforting aroma of her simple, timeless recipes fills the air. While the restaurant promises sophistication, sometimes nothing beats the warmth and reliability of grandma's cooking.

In Machine Learning, the choice between deep learning and simpler models follows a similar logic. Deep learning is undeniably powerful, capable of handling complex, unstructured data like images, audio, and natural language. However, its sophistication comes at a cost. Training a neural network requires immense computational power, often involving specialized hardware like GPUs or TPUs, and vast amounts of labeled data. Without these resources, deep learning models may struggle to deliver meaningful results, much like a Michelin dish falling flat without its exotic ingredients.

In contrast, simpler models like linear regression, decision trees, or even logistic regression thrive in scenarios where data is limited or well-structured. These models are computationally lightweight, faster to train, and easier to deploy. For instance, a decision tree might perform just as well, or even better, than a neural network when working with tabular data like customer transaction histories or medical records.

Another advantage of simpler models lies in their interpretability. Neural networks are often criticized as "black boxes," where understanding why a model made a specific decision is nearly impossible. This lack of transparency can be a serious drawback in fields like healthcare or finance, where decisions must be explainable and justifiable. Simpler algorithms, by contrast, provide clear decision paths or straightforward mathematical relationships, making them easier to debug, validate, and trust.

Finally, simpler models are often more robust. Deep learning models are prone to overfitting, especially with small datasets, and require careful tuning to generalize well. Simpler algorithms, with their limited capacity, naturally avoid this pitfall and may provide more consistent performance across different scenarios.

The bottom line? While deep learning can be transformative in the right conditions, it's not a one-size-fits-all solution. There are plenty of situations where the speed, simplicity, and reliability of traditional methods are the better choice, just like how grandma's tried-and-true recipes sometimes hit the spot better than luxury cuisine.

CHAPTER 6

AI Is Your Sixth Sense

One of my all-time favorite movies is *The Sixth Sense*. It's one of those rare films that combines suspense, surprise, and a touch of the super-natural to leave a lasting impression. The idea of having an extra sense—a hidden ability that lets you see things others can't—is both haunting and thrilling. Now, I don't expect AI to start revealing any ghosts around us (at least, I hope not!), but in many ways, AI can act as a sixth sense in our lives. It's a quiet, tireless partner that enhances our vision, perception, and intuition, revealing insights and patterns we might otherwise miss.

Imagine what it would be like to have this extra sense—a hidden ability that doesn't just complement our natural senses but enhances them. With AI as a partner, our own "sixth sense" becomes amplified, expanding the reach of our eyes, ears, and instincts. AI isn't just a tool; it's an ally that stands by, ready to help us make sense of a complex world.

In this chapter, we'll explore what it really means to have AI as a sixth sense by diving into the ways it can extend each of our basic senses. AI can act as your eyes, capturing and interpreting vast amounts of visual data to uncover details even the sharpest human eye might miss. It can serve as your ears and voice, listening to and interpreting language with an accuracy that rivals human comprehension. It can even oper-ate as your body, responding and adapting to experiences in real-time through trial and error, much like how we develop instincts.

And beyond that, AI can become your personal assistant, organizing and simplifying complex information at a speed that would take us ages to match. Finally, when one assistant isn't enough, AI can act as two teammates—collaborating, competing, and learning from each other to innovate in ways we've never imagined.

AI Is Your Eyes

Think of all the times you've relied on your vision to make quick judgments: spotting a friend in a crowd, scanning a report for key points, or even just recognizing familiar landmarks as you drive. Our eyes capture information at incredible speeds, but there's only so much detail we can take in at once. Now, imagine having an AI "sixth sense" that can enhance this vision, seeing deeper and detecting patterns faster than we ever could alone. This AI "super-vision" allows us to perceive the world in entirely new ways.

To understand how AI sees things, let's look at that popular game where you're shown a small corner of a zoomed-in picture of an object, and tiny portion is magnified hundreds of times. Your goal is to guess what it is. At first, you might only see a blur of colors or indistinct patterns—a patch of green, maybe some stripes. You can't identify the object right away. But as that viewable window slides from the corner to reveal more of the image, your mind combines each new detail with what you've already seen. Little by little, you use edges, textures, and colors as clues, piecing together the full picture until you suddenly recognize the object as, say, a tiger's eye or the surface of a leaf. This gradual process of layering insights is exactly how Convolutional Neural Networks, or CNNs, help AI "see."

CNNs use a similar approach, breaking down an image into layers of details. The network starts with broad filters to capture simple features, like colors or edges, much like how we first notice shapes and textures in a zoomed-in image. As more layers are added, the CNN's "vision" becomes increasingly refined. It detects more complex patterns like curves, shadows, or repeating textures—similar to how our minds process additional details until the full image clicks into place. By the end of this process, CNNs can combine all the small glimpses to form a clear, complete picture of the object.

Imagine CNNs at work in medical imaging, assisting doctors in analyzing X-rays or MRIs. It's like having an extra pair of tireless, super-powered eyes scanning those images. At the most basic level, the network might recognize edges and contrasts. Still, as it processes layer upon layer, it picks up more specific features: the shapes and textures of organs and the irregularities that might signify tumors or fractures.

Imagine an AI that can spot a tiny cluster of cancerous cells in a lung X-ray, something easily missed by the human eye, potentially saving a life through early detection. Just as you'd slowly recognize the image in the game, CNNs gradually learn to distinguish normal tissues from suspicious growths. This AI-powered sight can be remarkably accurate, often spotting details that might evade the human eye.

CNNs are also behind facial recognition software, like the kind you might use to unlock your smartphone. Think about how your phone unlocks just by glancing at it. When you lift your phone, CNNs analyze your face in stages, recognizing features like the distance between your eyes, the shape of your nose, and the curve of your mouth, layer by layer. It's similar to piecing together the whole image in the zoomed-in game, where each clue brings you closer to an answer. Thankfully, AI hasn't mastered judging us based on our bedhead morning selfies...yet!

But AI's vision goes far beyond what we can see with our own eyes. It's like having infrared vision, allowing it to detect people in the dark or identify faulty equipment in a factory through thermal imaging. Or imagine AI peering into the microscopic world, analyzing images at the cellular level to aid in disease diagnosis or materials science research. This "super-vision" allows us to perceive the world in entirely new ways.

With CNNs as our "eyes," AI becomes more than just a tool—it's an extension of our senses, able to detect features and patterns at scales beyond human capability. With AI by our side, we can see farther, deeper, and clearer than ever before, revealing a world full of hidden insights and possibilities.

AI Is Your Ears and Mouth

When you're deep in conversation with a friend, you're not just hearing their words; you're following the flow, understanding context, and responding thoughtfully. In a seamless exchange, your ears and mouth work together, turning sounds into meaning and meaning into responses. In the world of AI, these "ears and mouth" are combined not just metaphorically but also within the very architecture of Recurrent Neural Networks (RNNs). These networks are designed to both understand and generate language, mirroring the seamless flow of human conversation.

We link AI's "ears" and "mouth" because effective communication requires both simultaneously. Understanding what's been said is just the first step. AI must process this input, interpret its meaning, and then decide how to respond—all in real time, creating a smooth conversational flow. Much like how we listen and respond in a conversation, RNNs handle language as a dynamic exchange that requires memory of what's been said so far, an understanding of the context, and the ability to anticipate what comes next.

At the heart of this capability is the structure of RNNs, which makes them uniquely suited for processing sequences. Standard neural networks analyze data as isolated pieces, but RNNs have a kind of "memory." They remember what they've processed before, allowing them to build a sense of continuity and context with each new word or sound. Imagine reading a book: if you had to forget each sentence as soon as you moved to the next, you'd lose track of the story. RNNs overcome this by storing information from earlier in the sequence, crucial for understanding anything involving time, like conversations, music, or handwriting.

This "ears and mouth" capability allows AI to perform amazing feats of language processing. For example, you could be conversing with someone who speaks a different language, and your device seamlessly translates your words as you speak, allowing for natural, flowing dialogue. Or imagine automated closed captioning for live videos, making content accessible to everyone. This ability to understand language in context is also crucial for analyzing the sentiment behind customer reviews or social media posts.

Take virtual assistants like Siri or Alexa, for example. When you ask a question, RNNs act as the "ears" that interpret the sequence of words. But they don't just stop at understanding your question—they also use their "mouth" to generate a response that fits the context. If you say, "Remind me to buy milk," the assistant first listens, interpreting each word in the context of your query. Then, it "remembers" the context that you need a reminder and prepares a response that matches your request: "Got it! I'll remind you to buy milk." This back-and-forth requires the AI to listen, interpret, and respond in an ongoing sequence, combining the abilities of ears and mouth to create a seamless conversation.

The magic of RNNs lies in their ability to handle this flow. They are designed to analyze data sequentially, where each step depends on what's come before. But there's a bit of an art to it, too. Not only does an RNN need to remember recent inputs, but it must also weigh them correctly, distinguishing between critical details and background noise, focusing on what's relevant while setting aside what's not. This balance of memory and focus is essential for processing language. Imagine if a virtual assistant remembered every single word you'd ever said. Its responses would quickly become confusing or irrelevant. Instead, RNNs prioritize the most essential details, just as we do when listening closely.

Over time, researchers have developed even more sophisticated versions of RNNs that can remember longer sequences and handle more complex language tasks. AI can now hold more natural conversations, understand nuanced language, and generate creative text formats like poems or scripts.

In short, by combining the "ears" and "mouth" functions, AI becomes capable of more than just hearing or responding. It becomes a conversational partner that listens to you, understands what you mean, and responds thoughtfully—all in real time. With RNNs powering their language abilities, AI bridges the gap between passive listening and active conversation, becoming a more insightful, responsive partner in human communication.

AI Is Your Body

Think about learning a new skill, like riding a bike or playing a sport. At first, you rely on trial and error—falling, correcting your balance, adjusting your speed—until you gradually find the right balance and movements to stay steady. Over time, you develop the muscle memory, where your body intuitively knows what to do. In AI, Reinforcement Learning (RL) acts as this "body," allowing machines to learn from experience and refine their behaviors through feedback from their environment. It's like giving AI a "sixth sense" for navigating complex situations and making optimal decisions.

Reinforcement Learning is AI's version of trial and error. Just like a child learns not to touch a hot stove after a painful experience, an AI model learns through repeated attempts and feedback, developing an understanding of which actions lead to positive outcomes, and which don't.

The AI receives a reward when it makes a "good" decision and a penalty when it makes a "bad" one. The "rewards" in RL can take many forms. For a robot navigating a maze, the reward might be reaching the exit. For a financial trading model, the reward is profit. And for a personalized learning system, the reward could be the student's progress and understanding. Over time, this process of rewards and penalties shapes the AI's behavior, helping it learn the best way to accomplish a task.

Imagine a robot programmed to navigate a maze. At first, it might take random steps, hitting walls and running into dead ends. Each time it finds a clear path, it receives a small reward. When it reaches the exit, it gets a large reward. The robot's goal is to maximize its rewards, so over time, it begins to recognize which actions are more likely to lead it toward the exit. This feedback loop—trial, feedback, and adjustment—is the core of Reinforcement Learning. The robot's body learns to move more efficiently based on experiences, developing an "instinct" for reaching the goal faster and with fewer mistakes.

This idea of learning through interaction makes RL so powerful and versatile. Unlike traditional programming, where specific instructions are written for every possible scenario, RL allows AI to figure things out. It's often used in environments where outcomes are uncertain or dynamic, like teaching autonomous vehicles to navigate roads or training robots to adapt to new tasks. By learning from each encounter, the AI refines its responses until it operates with the efficiency and intuition of a practiced human.

In robotics, reinforcement learning helps machines perform physical tasks—like picking up objects, assembling products, or even helping in surgery. Just as we adapt our movements to improve over time, these robots adjust their actions based on real-time feedback, allowing them to work more efficiently. Imagine a warehouse robot learning to pick up delicate items without damaging them. At first, it might grip too tightly or too loosely, but with each attempt, it adjusts its strength and technique based on feedback. Over time, it learns the perfect grip for handling different items, achieving a kind of physical intuition for its task.

But RL isn't just about mechanical tasks. It's also used in environments where decision-making involves complex choices with uncertain outcomes. Take, for example, DeepMind's AlphaGo, which famously learned to play (and master) the complex board game Go through reinforcement learning. Instead of following pre-programmed strategies, AlphaGo learned by playing millions of games, adjusting its approach based on each win or loss. Through this constant feedback, strategies and moves were developed that human experts had never seen before.

By the time it competed against world champions, AlphaGo had not only "learned" the rules of the game but had evolved instincts and strategies that gave it a winning edge. It was as if it had built up its own muscle memory, understanding the moves that most often led to victory. This same principle applies to creating more dynamic and challenging opponents in video games. RL allows these virtual characters to adapt their strategies to your actions, making each playthrough a unique experience.

While RL is a powerful tool, it also has its challenges. Designing the right reward system can be tricky, and training can be time-consuming, especially for complex tasks. But despite these challenges, RL is pushing the boundaries of what AI can achieve, allowing machines to learn and adapt in ways that were once thought impossible.

Reinforcement Learning, in essence, turns AI into more than just a passive processor of information. It enables machines to engage with the world actively, adapting their actions based on feedback, building instincts, and becoming capable of handling complex tasks that demand more than simple calculations. It's AI as a "body" that learns and moves, adjusting its behavior to suit its environment. With reinforcement learning, AI takes on a whole new level of agency, discovering, adapting, and evolving in ways that make it a powerful partner in tasks that require real-world interaction.

AI Is Your Assistant

Picture an ideal assistant—a highly organized individual who can take a chaotic pile of papers and sort them into clear, neat files. This assistant is efficient, focused, and skilled at identifying what's essential while filtering out the unnecessary details. In the realm of AI, this kind of organized intelligence is powered by autoencoders, which help machines identify patterns, compress data, and make sense of complex information. An autoencoder's job is like that of an assistant who distills vast amounts of data into a simpler form, highlighting key insights and reducing information overload. Autoencoders provide a 'sixth sense' for recognizing patterns and anomalies hidden within complex data.

Autoencoders work by learning the essence of the data. They take in a lot of information, identify the most important features, and then create a simplified version. It's like creating a summary of a long document, capturing the key points while leaving out the unnecessary details. They are a type of neural network designed to learn efficient representations of data. Their purpose is to take in a complex set of inputs, process them to identify key features, and then reconstruct a simplified version of the original information.

You can think of it like organizing an overstuffed closet. An autoencoder might "compress" your wardrobe into categories, recognizing that five different T-shirts can be grouped together under "casual wear." By focusing on these patterns and categories, an autoencoder learns the structure of the data, becoming more efficient at identifying what's truly important.

One of the main tasks of an autoencoder is dimensionality reduction. Imagine you have thousands of photos of landscapes and want to organize them by common themes, like mountains, beaches, or forests. If you tried to compare every tiny pixel in every image, the process would be overwhelming. Instead, an autoencoder quickly identifies the main features—shapes, colors, textures—and organizes them into simplified representations. With this kind of high-level organization, it becomes much easier to search, analyze, or even enhance the images. The AI has, in effect, "decluttered" the data, making it easier to manage and interpret.

A powerful example of this in action is anomaly detection. In fields like cybersecurity, autoencoders can be trained to recognize the normal patterns of network activity. They learn what typical data looks like and compress it into a simplified format. But if an unusual pattern appears—say, a spike in network traffic or a sudden change in behavior—an autoencoder will notice that it doesn't match the usual compressed form. This discrepancy can signal an anomaly, like a potential cyberattack, that requires attention. It's as if your assistant were organizing your emails and flagged a suspicious message that didn't fit with the usual routine, alerting you before it could cause problems. Imagine an autoencoder monitoring credit card transactions. It learns the typical spending patterns of a user and can instantly flag unusual activity, like a sudden purchase in a foreign country, potentially preventing fraud.

In essence, autoencoders allow AI to perform as an organized, insightful assistant—one that excels at reducing complexity, uncovering patterns, and highlighting what's important. Just as an ideal assistant filters out distractions and helps you focus on the essentials, an autoencoder processes mountains of data, making it manageable and useful.

In a world flooded with information, this type of AI-driven assistance isn't just helpful; it's transformative, enabling us to see patterns, identify risks, and make decisions that would be difficult to achieve on our own. Imagine having an AI assistant that can sift through mountains of information and whisper the key insights directly to you – that's the power of autoencoders.

AI Is Your Assistant x 2

What's better than having an assistant? Having two assistants! And not just any assistant, but ones who actively challenge each other to improve, creating something better than either could alone. In the world of AI, Generative Adversarial Networks, or GANs, embody this concept perfectly. GANs are made up of two neural networks working in tandem: one as a creator (the generator) and the other as a critic (the discriminator). They engage in a competitive partnership, each pushing the other to excel and refine their work. GANs give AI a "sixth sense" for creativity and critical thinking, allowing it to generate and refine its own creations.

Think of GANs like a high-stakes cat-and-mouse game, similar to the dynamic between Leonardo DiCaprio's character, Frank Abagnale Jr., and Tom Hanks' character, Carl Hanratty, in *Catch Me If You Can*. (Yes, you can tell I am a big movie fan!) In the movie, Frank is a master forger who constantly devises ways to create false identities and documents. Carl, an FBI agent, is the relentless investigator who scrutinizes every move, learning to spot each forgery and forcing Frank to improve his techniques in order to avoid capture. Their back-and-forth creates an environment where each character hones their skills, refining their game with every encounter. In GANs, the generator is like Frank, constantly creating new "forgeries" of data, while the discriminator is like Carl, analyzing these forgeries to detect which are real and which are fake.

Here's how this partnership works: the generator, like Frank, starts by creating data samples that resemble real ones. Imagine it generating fake images of faces that look as realistic as possible. The discriminator, like Carl, receives these images and examines them closely, trying to distinguish the real ones from the fakes. It's like the ultimate fact-checker, making sure the generator doesn't get away with any 'fake news' in the data world. If it spots any flaws—anything that reveals the generator's "forgery"—it sends this feedback to the generator, who adjusts its methods to create even more convincing images. Over time, just as Frank becomes better at creating believable identities, the generator improves its ability to produce images so realistic that they become almost indistinguishable from actual photos.

This cycle of competition and collaboration between the generator and the discriminator creates a powerful feedback loop. The generator learns from its mistakes, adapting to each new layer of scrutiny the discriminator provides. Meanwhile, the discriminator sharpens its own abilities, continually finding more subtle ways to detect even the smallest hints of forgery. Just like how Carl becomes more adept at spotting Frank's clever tricks, the discriminator grows more skilled at identifying details that signal a fake, forcing the generator to innovate.

The magic of GANs lies in this tension. By challenging each other, the generator and discriminator produce results that neither could achieve alone. This dual-assistant structure has revolutionized AI's ability to generate realistic data, creating stunning results in fields like art, photography, and even video game design. For instance, GANs can generate hyper-realistic images of people, places, or objects that don't exist in the real world. From fake human faces that look creepily authentic to imaginary landscapes that could pass for photos, GANs create visuals that seem real to the naked eye—all thanks to the constant back-and-forth between these two "assistants." GANs are not just about analyzing existing data; they can generate entirely new data that has never existed before. This opens up incredible possibilities for creating realistic simulations, generating personalized content, and even imagining entirely new worlds.

Beyond just image generation, GANs are also used in areas like data augmentation, where they generate synthetic data to train other AI models. For example, in medical research, GANs can create realistic samples of rare medical conditions to help train diagnostic algorithms, making it easier for AI to identify these conditions in real patients. This way, the dual-assistant system isn't just creating convincing images—it's contributing valuable training material to improve other AI applications. Imagine an AI with the intuition of a master artist and the discerning eye of a seasoned critic – that's the power of GANs.

The relationship between GANs' generator and discriminator goes far beyond mere creation and critique. It's a creative partnership, where both sides push each other to reach new heights, producing results that blur the lines between reality and artificiality. Just like Frank and Carl in *Catch Me If You Can*, their rivalry doesn't end with a "winner" or "loser." Instead, it leads to a form of mutual growth, where each gains something from the other. In the end, AI with GANs is more than just an assistant—it's a collaborative duo that combines creative generation with critical analysis, redefining what machines can create.

As we've seen, AI can extend our senses and abilities, from seeing and listening to thinking, acting, and even creating in ways that enhance our daily lives. With AI as our sixth sense, we gain a powerful partner that sees patterns, learns from experience, and even collaborates with itself to push the boundaries of creativity and insight. But beyond technical prowess, our relationship with AI is evolving. It's not just about functionality—it's about trust, understanding, and mutual benefit.

But how do we build trust with something that seems so different from us? How do we navigate the ethical dilemmas that arise when AI becomes deeply integrated into our lives? These are the questions we'll explore in the next chapter.

CHAPTER 7

Dating with AI

They say names are fate. So perhaps it was inevitable that a guy named Cupid would end up writing about relationships—although I never imagined it would involve Artificial Intelligence! Maybe I should have seen it coming, though. After all, who needs arrows and doves when you have algorithms and neural networks? But here we are, exploring the quirks, challenges, and promise of what's become one of humanity's most *unique* relationships: our growing connection with AI. It's a relationship unlike any other, where we're learning to interact with a form of intelligence that's both familiar and profoundly different from our own.

While it may not involve candlelit dinners, roses, or chocolate, our relationship with AI has all the complexity of a classic romance, complete with first impressions, trust issues, and deciding whether to tie the knot. When you think about it, forming a relationship with AI isn't so different from getting to know a new friend or potential romantic partner. We encounter AI in many aspects of our lives—from the algorithms that recommend movies to us to the virtual assistants that respond to our voices—and, just like any first date, we're still figuring each other out. Sometimes, we're swept off our feet by what AI can do; other times, we might feel unsettled by how much it seems to know about us. And, like any relationship worth having, this one requires trust, open communication, and mutual respect.

So, let's dive in! After all, it seems that Cupid has struck again—just this time, with an AI in a bow. By the end of this chapter, we'll have a better sense of navigating this "dating" adventure with AI, bringing us closer to a productive, balanced, and, hopefully, mutually beneficial relationship.

First Impressions Matter: Understanding Bias in AI

When you meet someone for the first time, it's easy to form a quick impression based on surface details—appearance, initial words, or even what you've heard about them. Sometimes, these first impressions are spot-on; other times, they're way off. AI systems are no different in this regard: they, too, make judgments based on what they "see" in data. Just as we might make assumptions about someone on a first date based on their clothes or how they speak, AI systems can also form biased "first impressions" based on the data they're trained on. But unlike us, AI has no independent judgment. It learns from the data we feed it—data that, in many cases, reflects our patterns, preferences, and, yes, even our biases.

This leads us to an interesting point: if AI exhibits bias, we may need to look in the mirror first. Just as a child's behavior often reflect the environment they grow up in, AI mirrors the biases embedded in the data it's trained on. Imagine a parent who frequently curses, telling their child not to use foul language. Despite the words, the child might think, "Well, if they do it, it must be okay." Similarly, if we're feeding AI data that contains stereotypes, biases, or prejudiced viewpoints, we shouldn't be too surprised when AI begins to reflect them on us.

Bias in AI is particularly tricky because it's usually unintentional. AI learns from vast amounts of data—text, images, and videos—all generated by us. And even when we try to be fair, historical or societal biases can seep into the data. For instance, if an AI model is trained to recognize professionals in photos but most images depict men in certain roles and women in others, it might start associating job types with specific genders. This is not because AI is "prejudiced" but because it has internalized patterns based on our examples. It's simply echoing back the biases it's learned. Imagine a language model trained on text from the internet. It might learn to associate certain words or phrases with specific genders or ethnicities, leading to biased language generation.

The consequences of biased AI can be far-reaching. When bias becomes part of the "first impression" an AI system forms, it can influence everything from hiring algorithms to loan approvals and criminal justice decisions. Imagine applying for a job where the initial resume is screened by an AI trained on historical hiring data that favors specific backgrounds over others. This could lead to unjust rejections based on characteristics unrelated to a candidate's abilities, reinforcing biases and inequalities rather than breaking them down. Biased AI can perpetuate harmful stereotypes, limit opportunities for certain groups, and even lead to discrimination in critical areas like healthcare, education, and the justice system. Addressing these biases is crucial to ensure that AI is used fairly and ethically.

Fortunately, we're not without options. Just as we can correct our assumptions and learn to look beyond surface impressions, we can actively work to make AI fairer. One way to tackle this is by diversifying the data we feed AI systems, ensuring that it reflects a broader, more balanced perspective. Another way is to develop algorithms that identify and correct bias in real-time, which allows AI systems to "self-reflect" in a sense, just as we do when we catch ourselves making unfair assumptions.

Ultimately, building fairer AI requires more than just technological fixes. It also calls for a degree of humility on our part—a willingness to recognize that AI's biases are often our own, reflected in us. By addressing these biases at the source, we're not only creating more ethical AI systems but also encouraging a more inclusive perspective in ourselves. And just as in human relationships, the effort to see beyond first impressions can lead to more meaningful connections—both with each other and with AI.

A real-world example of AI bias surfaced when Amazon developed a machine-learning-based recruiting tool starting in 2014. They have a good intention to streamline the hiring process by automatically evaluating resumes. However, the system soon began favoring male candidates over women. This bias emerged because the algorithm was trained on historical hiring data - data that reflected an already male-dominated tech industry. Although Amazon tried to correct these imbalances by tweaking the tool's algorithms, they eventually scrapped the project upon realizing that subtle new forms of bias could still persist. This highlights a core issue raised earlier: even with the best intentions when AI has trained on data embedding historical or societal inequalities, its "first impressions" can perpetuate and amplify those same biases in the real world.

The responsibility for creating fair and unbiased AI lies with us. We must be mindful of the data we use, the algorithms we design, and the potential impact of our creations. By taking proactive steps to address bias, we can ensure that AI is a force for good in the world.

The Overprotective Partner: When AI Just Won't Stop Checking In

Early in a relationship, a little extra attention can feel flattering. But what if your new partner starts checking in every hour, tracking your location, or knowing your plans before you share them? That's when "just checking in" crosses a line into something that feels less like affection and more like surveillance. It's like we're dating an AI who is *too* keen on knowing our every move. AI constantly monitors, collects, and stores details about us—sometimes beyond what we realize or are comfortable with. Just as a partner who constantly monitors can make us feel like our privacy is compromised, AI's pervasive surveillance can feel invasive, too.

Take facial recognition, for example. This technology is becoming as common as a phone lock screen, allowing for quick access or the convenience of automated check-ins at airports. However, the same technology that recognizes us can also track us without our knowledge, compiling an unending stream of information about our movements, interactions, and habits. Imagine going on a date, and your new partner keeps taking pictures of you without asking, even when you're not looking. That's what unchecked facial recognition can feel like.

Voice assistants add another layer to this ever-present AI. They listen, often continuously, waiting for their "wake word." And while we appreciate how easily they respond when we ask for directions or play music, they can also hear far more than we intend. Consider the snippets of conversations they might catch—anything from private discussions to mundane background chatter. It's like having a partner who hears all your mutterings, private talks, and even background noises, logging data without filtering what's relevant to the "relationship."

This constant data collection isn't just a passing phase; it builds a digital profile of us over time. Every online purchase, every social media post, every Google search—it's all saved, analyzed, and sometimes shared. While this data can enable AI to "know" us better and offer personalized recommendations, it can also leave us feeling exposed. In the same way that a partner who knows every personal detail can make us feel overpowered or even vulnerable, AI's ability to collect vast amounts of information can make us uneasy, as if we're losing control over our own narrative. This constant surveillance can erode our sense of freedom and autonomy. It can lead to discrimination, manipulation, and even social control. In a world where our every move is tracked and analyzed, it becomes difficult to be ourselves.

The concept of "consent" gets murky here, too. In human relationships, boundaries are discussed and respected—ideally, both partners agree on what's shared and kept private. But with AI, we often aren't fully aware of the extent of data we consent to share. The fine print on terms and conditions might reveal some details, but who has the time to read pages of legalese? Most people end up granting broad permissions without realizing it, giving AI full access to our "private lives" without explicit, meaningful consent.

This overprotective AI "partner" can even start making assumptions about us—similar to a partner who might think they know what's best for you based on patterns they observe. AI might notice you've been searching for home improvement ideas, and suddenly, every ad and suggestion nudges you toward home products, even if you were just curious. These nudges can shape our decisions and preferences, sometimes subtly guiding us in ways that may not reflect our real needs or desires. AI's surveillance and data-driven predictions might be intended to serve us, but it often feels as though our choices are no longer entirely our own.

As in any relationship, setting boundaries with AI is essential to maintain autonomy and respect for our personal space. Privacy settings, encrypted communications, and mindful data-sharing practices are like setting boundaries with that over-involved partner. Tools to limit data tracking, opting out of invasive data collection, and questioning when and where AI is observing us are ways to ensure AI respects our privacy.

A recent example underscores this very concern: Apple—often celebrated for its focus on privacy—agreed to pay $95 million to settle a lawsuit alleging that its virtual assistant, Siri, recorded users without their explicit consent. The lawsuit claimed Siri occasionally activated itself even without the "Hey, Siri" trigger, capturing snippets of private conversations and potentially sharing them for targeted advertising. Although Apple denies any wrongdoing and insists it never sold user data for marketing, this settlement points to the complexities of AI-enabled devices. Even for a company that publicly champions consumer privacy, subtle design choices or technical oversights can inadvertently turn a supposedly helpful feature into an invasive, over-listening entity. It's a reminder that transparency, explicit consent, and rigorous data protections remain paramount as AI grows increasingly entwined with our daily lives.

Just as we would set boundaries with a human partner, we need to set boundaries with AI. This means being mindful of the data we share, adjusting privacy settings on our devices, and supporting regulations that protect our digital rights. We must make it clear to our AI 'partner' that we value our privacy and autonomy. Striking a balance between AI's helpful insights and our comfort with its knowledge of our lives will make AI feel like a supportive partner rather than an overbearing one. Ultimately, a respectful relationship—whether with a person or an intelligent system—requires open communication and a willingness to respect boundaries. And as AI becomes increasingly embedded in our lives, finding ways to manage that relationship thoughtfully is as essential as ever.

Yours, Mine, or Ours? Untangling Data Ownership in the AI Era

As our relationship with AI evolves, so do questions about shared belongings and personal space. Is it "yours," "mine," or "ours"? With AI, data ownership isn't just a matter of privacy or control—it's also about who truly has a claim to the information we generate every day. Is it our data because it's our personal information? Or does it belong to the tech companies collecting, processing, and storing it? And in cases where our data contributes to AI's "knowledge," are we entitled to any ownership of the insights or models built from it?

Data is often likened to a resource—a raw material like oil or gold. But unlike physical resources, data is deeply personal, and it exists in the form of digital traces: our clicks, our searches, our location history, and the things we like and share. These traces create a digital identity that's uniquely ours, yet it's not under our exclusive control. Most platforms collect and aggregate our data as a trade-off for services we enjoy—recommendations, social connections, and personalized experiences. Yet, when it comes to deciding who owns this data, things get tricky. Who has the right to use, sell, or delete these bits of our lives? It's like bringing your prized possessions into a relationship and then realizing you're not sure who gets to keep them if things don't work out.

This question is so complex because AI systems don't just use data—they depend on it to learn, improve, and create value. Imagine someone whose personality is shaped by absorbing parts of everyone they meet. Similarly, an AI model's "intelligence" is formed by aggregating vast amounts of individual data. This raises a question: if our data helps create a highly profitable or impactful AI model, should we have any claim to that model? Or is it solely the company's property that built and trained it? Imagine your partner learning all your secrets and then using that knowledge to create something valuable without giving you credit. This issue touches on more than just ethical considerations; it has real implications for ownership, compensation, and control.

The ambiguity around data ownership often benefits companies. Terms of service agreements typically grant them broad rights to collect and use data, but the details are usually hidden in lengthy, jargon-filled docu-ments. Many people agree to these terms without fully understanding them, essentially "sharing" their data without realizing that they may also be giving away ownership rights. It's a bit like signing a lease for an apart-ment only to discover later that, by signing, you've given the landlord the right to make copies of your house keys and visit whenever they like.

This isn't only a matter of access but also of purpose. Data about us might start as harmless demographic or behavioral information used to improve a product or personalize our experience. However, as companies develop more sophisticated AI over time, they can mine this data for insights that might reveal even more about us than we intended to share. These insights can be used to influence our decisions, recommend products, or even predict our future behavior, all without us having a say in how it's done.

The debate over data ownership is heating up as people become more aware of the value of their information. New questions are emerging: Should individuals have a right to be compensated when their data helps train valuable AI models? Should data creators—individual users— be granted more power to control, restrict, or even withdraw their data after it's been shared?

Advocates for stronger data rights argue that individuals should have more transparency, if not outright ownership, over their personal infor-mation. Others propose solutions allowing people to "license" their data rather than giving it away permanently, creating a model more similar to royalties than outright ownership. Imagine forming a 'data union' with other users to collectively negotiate with companies about how our data is used and compensated.

The lack of clear ownership standards also affects trust in AI. Without clear boundaries, people can feel like they're losing control over parts of themselves, leading to suspicion and resentment. Just as in any relationship, ownership and trust go hand in hand. When we don't feel secure in our claim to something uniquely ours, like our data, it's hard to trust that it's being used responsibly.

As AI continues to evolve, society must address these issues more directly. While there's no easy answer to data ownership, we may eventually arrive at models recognizing individuals' digital identity rights while allowing innovation to flourish. The rules around data ownership are still being written. As AI becomes more sophisticated and integrated into our lives, we need to have open and honest conversations about balancing individual rights with AI innovation's potential benefits.

These questions of "who owns what" become particularly charged in the creative industry. Tools like DALL·E and Stable Diffusion offer near-instant artwork generation from a few lines of text - anything from a surreal astronaut surfing in Times Square to a lawyer unwinding on a sunny beach. While this technology democratizes art-making and sparks innovation, it also raises complex authorship issues: Is the creator the user typing the prompt, or is the AI that assembles the image from countless data points - often derived from existing, potentially copyrighted works? If an AI-generated image bears a striking resemblance to a living artist's style or a copyrighted logo, does the user risk legal repercussions for infringement? These gray areas of co-authorship, credit, and commercialization highlight the fundamental need for more precise rules around data use and ownership - especially as AI learns from vast, collective repositories of human creativity to produce digital works that might occupy a legal limbo.

The future of our relationship with AI depends on finding a fair and equitable solution to the data ownership question. Until then, however, we find ourselves in a complicated, undefined space: navigating the blurred lines of "yours," "mine," and "ours" in the digital world and wondering if our data is genuinely still our own.

Can I Trust You? Building Transparency in Our 'Black Box' Relationship with AI

In any relationship, trust is essential. But trust doesn't come easily when we don't understand what's happening on the other side. It's like being in a relationship where your partner makes all the decisions without explaining their reasoning. You might wonder if they genuinely have your best interests at heart. In the world of AI, this feeling of uncertainty is common.

Some friends in medicine have expressed concerns about AI's role in healthcare: "AI is a black box and hence untrustable."

Is that true? If you look around, there are many more black boxes in other areas, but we are still okay with using them because we are so used to them. How many people truly understand how an aircraft works before they fly?

"... [But] if I ask an aerospace engineer about flying, she can explain the theory and specifics. When I asked the AI engineer how we would evaluate the recommendations of the ML/DL they had set loose for the algorithm, he said that the results speak for themselves and he didn't need to understand how or why. That answer bothered me..." they further elaborated.

A black box is something you cannot see what happens inside. However, as opposed to what a black box is, all AI algorithms are literally the result of combining calculus, statistics, probability, and mathematics, and humans have studied those areas for many years. AI is a new approach that creatively combines those disciplines. We can know exactly how those AI models behave and explain that bit-by-bit and step-by-step "mathematically and statistically." AI just performs well-defined mathematical operations with data as the input and the model as the output.

What we are missing here is the explanation in the high-level context that humans can comprehend. Let's say I love purple, and I am happy to see my stuff in that color (the benefit of the result of AI). However, I cannot explain why, but I just love it. This feeling of love, when broken down to a very low level, is the light energy received by the retina in my eyes, which then be converted to the signal sent to my brain and triggers some special neurons to make me feel happy (calculus, statistics, probability, and mathematics).

Can I say my feeling of loving purple is not real and un-trustable because I cannot explain why I have that pleasing feeling in high-level terms? Or shall I accept the fact that I love this color, acknowledging that this is the combining result of lower-level physics, chemistry, and biology?

"I know you love AI technology, but there is a real risk to AI in healthcare. It will continue to underperform what was promised," my dear friend and respectful doctor said.

AI has a long way to go before matching up with a qualified expert. However, few people perform at the quality level they think they do because of genuine incapability or physical constraints, such as a lack of sleep. In those cases, AI can complement. Though a black box lacks a high-level understanding, its performance is undeniably tested and proven by hard-cold numbers.

In the healthcare context, trust becomes even more critical. As Quinn and colleagues point out in their article on "Trust and medical AI," (PMCID: PMC7973477) the consequences of AI underperformance or failure aren't limited to suboptimal clinical outcomes; they can also erode public confidence in healthcare institutions. This erosion occurs when black-box models yield biased or opaque recommendations, when cybersecurity threats compromise patient privacy, or when clinical staff lack the training to interpret AI outputs responsibly. I agree with what Quinn's team underscores about the need for specialized expert groups—developers, validators, and operational staff—to handle the conceptual, technical, and humanistic complexities of AI in medicine. Their proposed solution includes formal education and accreditation in "digital medicine" so professionals can align AI tools with patient-centered care, ethical principles, and robust governance. By adopting such measures, the healthcare industry can mitigate risks, foster transparency, and retain the trust that underpins successful medical practice.

Transparency isn't about opening every door in AI's decision-making process; it's about finding meaningful ways to explain how AI reaches its conclusions so that people can understand and trust those decisions. While we strive for transparency, it's essential to recognize that some AI systems are so complex that even experts struggle to understand their inner workings fully. This is an ongoing challenge for the field. But to be fair, this is also true for any field if you go deep enough, but not only limited to AI. Despite that, we should keep finding ways to open more of this black box for better transparency, which can lead to broader adoption of AI and, ultimately, a more harmonious relationship between humans and this powerful technology.

Truth or Trick? Spotting the Deceptive AI Partner

Imagine being in a relationship with someone who is so convincing that you can't always tell when they're being genuine. This is the dilemma AI presents with its growing ability to create hyper-realistic but entirely fabricated content. Whether it's a deepfake video, a fabricated news story, or a manipulated image, AI has become capable of producing media that's almost impossible to distinguish from reality. This isn't a question of understanding AI's decision-making process—it's about AI becoming so good at mimicking reality that it's difficult, if not impossible, to identify what's real and what's artificial.

This ability to deceive has far-reaching consequences. In the past, a photo or video was considered credible evidence, but AI-generated content undermines that trust. For example, a hyper-realistic deepfake video showing a public figure making controversial statements could go viral, swaying public opinion before the truth is revealed. This power to deceive on a large scale puts AI in a position to not only alter individual perceptions but also influence societal beliefs, creating a new kind of information crisis.

What makes this especially challenging is the speed at which AI-generated misinformation spreads. In today's digital landscape, AI-powered algorithms quickly pick up on engaging content and amplify it across social networks. A fabricated story or video doesn't just reach a few people—it can reach millions within minutes, creating a tidal wave of misinformation before fact-checkers can intervene. Like a partner who strategically chooses their words to play on your emotions, AI-generated content can manipulate, mislead, and distort reality in ways that feel disturbingly personal.

This is a complex issue because AI can generate content that resonates with specific audiences. Through highly personalized recommendations, AI often shows us information that aligns with our pre-existing beliefs and biases. While this makes our online experience feel tailored to us, it also risks creating "echo chambers," where we're surrounded by content that reinforces our views, whether accurate or not. This effect can amplify misinformation, making AI-generated content seem even more credible because it aligns perfectly with what we already believe or want to believe.

Addressing this issue requires new tools and standards for identifying AI-generated content. Some companies and researchers are working on technologies that can detect deepfakes or verify the authenticity of images and videos, but this is an ongoing challenge. Knowing when AI has created or modified a piece of media gives us the context to evaluate it more carefully, helping us distinguish truth from trickery.

Ultimately, AI's ability to deceive reminds us to approach digital information critically. As AI becomes more adept at creating convincing fakes, our relationship with information must evolve. Just as in a relationship where we learn to recognize signs of sincerity or deception, we must develop similar instincts and tools to assess AI-generated content. In this way, we can create a future where AI's capabilities enhance truth rather than obscure it, maintaining a balanced and honest relationship with this powerful technology.

Tie the Knot, or Not? Evaluating Safety and Reliability in AI

Taking the next step in a relationship can be scary. It's like deciding whether to get married. You have to be sure your partner is reliable and trustworthy and won't do anything to put you in danger. Sometimes, it's not like your partner intentionally tricks you, as we discussed in the previous section, but they are incapable of fulfilling the promise they made to you.

We face a similar dilemma with AI. Deciding to fully integrate AI technology into our lives, institutions, and even critical sectors like healthcare and finance demands confidence in its reliability and safety. Just as we wouldn't commit to a partner, we couldn't trust to show up consistently, the choice to rely on AI requires a similar level of assurance.

AI's capabilities make it an appealing "partner" across a range of fields, from autonomous vehicles to medical diagnosis and financial decision-making. Yet, its safety and reliability are still areas of debate. Unlike more predictable tools, AI doesn't simply follow rigid instructions. Instead, it learns from vast datasets, meaning its "behavior" can be hard to predict. It's like dating someone full of surprises. Sometimes, those surprises are delightful, but sometimes, they can be unsettling. We need to know that AI won't suddenly do something unexpected that could harm us. However, in high-stakes applications, even a minor miscalculation or small error can have serious consequences, raising questions about whether AI is ready for this level of commitment.

AI, at its core, is just a tool—neutral by nature, with its actions shaped by those who use it. Like a car, which can offer us convenience and mobility, the potential can be misused. Human choices and intentions ultimately determine AI's role. Many of us rely on cars for everyday tasks and don't consider banning them simply because they could be used harmfully in the wrong hands. Similarly, AI's utility should not disappear just because it has risks; instead, our responsibility is to handle it thoughtfully, manage the risks, and direct its use toward beneficial ends.

When we look at AI as a potential long-term "partner," we need robust testing, accountability, and oversight to ensure it's safe and reliable. Before fully integrating AI into critical roles, we must rigorously test its performance across various situations, including edge cases where errors could be costly. It's like a trial period in a relationship, where we see how our partner handles different situations and challenges. Just as a marriage requires ongoing work and mutual commitment, our relationship with AI must involve continuous evaluation and improvement to ensure it adapts safely and effectively over time.

Of course, some skeptics argue that AI is too unpredictable to rely on, especially in areas like healthcare, where nuanced, life-or-death decisions are involved. AI indeed lacks the judgment and intuition of a human expert, which can lead to failures in cases requiring empathy, ethics, or nuanced decision-making. A doctor, for instance, might notice subtle cues in a patient that an AI could overlook or might consider factors that can't be distilled into data. While AI's decisions are powerful, they lack a human touch that can be critical in sensitive contexts.

Despite these limitations, AI can still be a valuable "assistant" in the relationship, complementing human strengths rather than replacing them. In healthcare, for example, AI can scan thousands of records in seconds to identify patterns, saving doctors time and reducing cognitive load. In finance, it can monitor market trends in real-time, catching changes that a human might miss. By working alongside human experts, AI provides support that can improve outcomes without assuming the full responsibility of the decision-making process. Therefore, I think the proper name for AI should be "Augmented" Intelligence instead of "Artificial" Intelligence.

Concerns around control are also part of this conversation. As AI becomes more integrated into society, there's a worry that we could lose control over its decisions, especially as it learns and adapts. It's understandable to feel anxious about the growing power of AI. But it's important to remember that we are still in control. We are the ones who design, develop, and deploy AI systems. We have the power to shape its future and ensure that it aligns with our values and goals. The key is to be proactive and responsible in our approach to AI development. However, this fear often overlooks AI's essential nature: it's still a tool we design, direct, and improve. Like any tool, it's up to us to use it responsibly and retain control. With proper safeguards, AI can remain a helpful partner without becoming a loose cannon.

So, is AI ready to "tie the knot" with society and take on these critical roles? It's still an evolving relationship rather than a full commitment. Navigating our relationship with AI requires an ongoing conversation. We must bring diverse perspectives together to address the ethical challenges, develop safeguards, and ensure that AI benefits humanity. This is not a journey we can undertake alone. It requires collaboration and a shared commitment to building a future where AI is a force for good.

As we continue to improve AI's reliability and transparency, we're moving closer to a future where it may be safe to let AI handle more significant responsibilities. But as in any relationship, it's wise to proceed cautiously, communicate openly, and continually reassess whether we're ready for a more profound commitment. The decision to "tie the knot" with AI is ultimately about our willingness to manage it thoughtfully, ensuring it serves us safely and reliably as we navigate this partnership.

CHAPTER 8

Pushing Boundaries: The New Wave of AI Breakthroughs and Beyond

As we saw in previous chapters, AI is no longer a futuristic fantasy; it's here. Understanding its foundation and how it relates to us is just the beginning. A new wave of AI innovation is upon us, pushing the boundaries of what's possible and redefining our relationship with this technology.

This chapter will explore the latest AI breakthroughs built on the foundation we saw earlier. Some of these innovations are natural extensions, and some tackle specific concerns we discussed; both are pushing the boundaries. Join us as we explore the exciting possibilities and navigate the complex landscape of this new era of AI.

Generative AI: Unlocking Creativity Through Machines

The creative spark is no longer solely a human domain. Generative AI has ignited a revolution, empowering machines to produce original content that rivals human ingenuity. From stunning visuals and captivating stories to melodies that stir the soul, generative AI redefines the boundaries of creative expression.

Rather than simply analyzing data or identifying patterns, generative AI takes it further by producing novel outputs that resemble human creativity. This leap forward has fueled innovations across industries: marketing teams generate personalized ad content, artists explore new forms of expression, and engineers experiment with product designs—all with the help of generative AI.

How Does It Work?

The magic behind generative AI lies in two main types of models: Generative Adversarial Networks (GANs) and Transformer-based models like the GPT (Generative Pre-trained Transformer) series. As we saw in an earlier chapter, GANs operate with two networks in a dynamic inter-play: a generator that creates content and a discriminator that evaluates its authenticity. Over time, the generator improves, learning to create increasingly realistic outputs that fool even the discerning discriminator. This setup has been particularly powerful for generating lifelike images, video, and 3D content.

Meanwhile, transformer-based models like GPT, BERT, and their successors have revolutionized text generation. Trained on massive datasets, these models learn complex patterns in language, enabling them to respond to prompts, write essays, or even mimic specific writing styles. Transformers' capability to capture intricate language dependencies has made text generation far more coherent and contextual, fueling applications in chatbots, customer support, and content creation.

Where Can It Apply To?

Text and Content Creation: Generative AI has quickly become a versatile content creator, from writing articles and generating code to crafting personalized emails. It helps streamline repetitive tasks, freeing human writers and designers for more strategic work. For example, generative AI can create compelling and unique descriptions for thousands of products in minutes instead of spending hours writing descriptions for an online store.

Image and Video Synthesis: GANs frequently create realistic images, alter videos, or enhance low-quality visuals. This has enabled applications in advertising, entertainment, and virtual reality, where high-quality synthetic visuals are essential. Generative AI can also create personalized avatars for video games, generate realistic special effects for movies, or even reconstruct damaged historical photographs. Notable examples include DeepArt, which turns photos into stylistic art, and deepfake technology, which, while controversial, demonstrates the realistic video alterations that generative AI can achieve.

Design and Prototyping: Generative AI offers new ways to explore forms and ideas in architecture, fashion, and product design. AI-generated prototypes allow designers to experiment with unique concepts rapidly, helping them find solutions they may not have envisioned. Architects can use generative AI to explore countless design variations for a new building, optimizing for aesthetics, energy efficiency, and structural integrity. Fashion brands, for instance, can use generative AI to experiment with patterns and materials, while automotive designers test out innovative shapes and finishes.

Healthcare and Drug Discovery: Generative AI is also impacting scientific fields. In drug discovery, AI can help identify potential new molecules and compounds, accelerating the development of new medications. This capability saves time and resources, making it feasible to evaluate countless chemical combinations before entering a lab.

What are the Challenges?

As the last chapter mentioned, establishing a relationship with AI presents some issues. Generative AI amplifies some of those with all its potential and brings unique challenges and ethical issues. One of the major concerns is data bias, as generative models often inherit biases from the datasets they're trained on, which can lead to biased outputs. If an AI model trained in art predominantly reflects Western styles, it may not generate works that authentically represent non-Western aesthetics. Addressing these biases requires careful dataset curation and continual model evaluation.

Misuse and misinformation are also significant risks. Generative AI can create deepfakes or synthetic content indistinguishable from reality, raising concerns about misinformation, privacy, and security. While deepfake technology is sometimes used for entertainment, it has sparked debate over its potential for spreading false information and violating privacy rights.

Finally, there is the issue of intellectual property (IP) and ownership. When an AI creates art, music, or written content, who owns the work—the AI creator, the user, or the company behind the AI? As generative AI produces more content, questions about rights and originality arise, sparking legal and ethical debates about the ownership of AI-generated work.

As Uncle Ben advises the young Peter Parker, Spider-Man: "With great power comes great responsibility." Generative AI, one of the most powerful tools in the AI family, has already reshaped multiple industries and should carry much more weight to be responsible. Balancing its transformative power with ethical safeguards will be vital to ensuring that generative AI continues to enrich society responsibly.

Large Language Models (LLMs): Powering the Language of AI

Among all types of Generative AI, Large Language Models (LLMs) is the most influential type at the time of this writing. The words we speak, the stories we write, and the very essence of human communication are all revolutionized by the rise of it. These powerful AI systems are mastering the nuances of language, enabling machines to converse, create, and comprehend with unprecedented fluency.

At the heart of today's generative AI boom is this powerful technology. LLMs, such as GPT (Generative Pre-trained Transformer) by OpenAI, BERT by Google, and their counterparts, have fundamentally changed how machines process and understand language. With the ability to generate human-like text, answer complex questions, and even create engaging dialogue, LLMs are reshaping fields from customer service to creative writing. Leading the charge in AI-powered language, LLMs are versatile, influential, and sometimes surprisingly conversational, making them one of the most transformative innovations in Artificial Intelligence.

How Does It Work?

Large Language Models are a category of transformer-based AI models trained on vast text datasets, often pulled from diverse sources across the internet, books, articles, and more. They use transformer architectures, which excel at understanding language by mapping relationships between words and phrases across multiple contexts. Imagine reading a sentence where the meaning depends on the relationship between words that are far apart. LLMs have a unique ability to 'connect the dots' between these words, no matter where they appear in the text. This is like having a superpower that allows you to instantly grasp the meaning of complex sentences, even if the words are jumbled up.

Another defining feature of LLMs is their sheer size. These models have billions of parameters and variables that they adjust during training to understand patterns and associations in the data. For instance, GPT-4, an

LLM by OpenAI, has over one trillion parameters, making it one of the largest and most capable language models at its release. The enormous size of these models enables them to generate detailed, coherent, and contextually relevant responses, but it also requires extensive computational resources for both training and deployment.

Where Can It Apply To?

Conversational AI and Chatbots: One of the most visible applications of LLMs is conversational AI, where they serve as the brains behind chatbots and virtual assistants. Imagine a chatbot that can not only answer your questions about a product but also understand your emotions and respond with empathy and understanding. LLMs are making this a reality. By generating coherent, natural-sounding responses, LLMs enable businesses to provide instant customer support, answer frequently asked questions, and even troubleshoot issues with a level of responsiveness that mimics a human touch.

Content Creation and Summarization: LLMs are also transforming content creation. They have become valuable tools for writers and marketers, from drafting blog posts to summarizing lengthy articles. Instead of spending hours researching and writing a report, you could use an LLM to quickly summarize key findings from multiple documents and even generate different sections of the report in various writing styles. For instance, businesses can use LLMs to generate ad copy, while researchers rely on them to distill complex information into concise summaries. In fields like journalism, LLMs can assist in summarizing news stories or even drafting initial reports, allowing professionals to work faster without compromising quality.

Code Generation and Assistance: Recognizing the demand for programming support, AI developers have fine-tuned LLMs to understand and generate code. LLMs can help translate code from one programming language to another, making it easier for developers to collaborate and share their work. Models like OpenAI's Codex can generate functional code snippets, debug programming errors, or even recommend best practices. This capability is helping both seasoned developers and beginners write code more efficiently, breaking down barriers in software development and increasing productivity in the tech industry.

Language Translation and Localization: LLMs are making strides in language translation, allowing businesses to expand their global reach. By adapting phrases to local dialects and nuances, LLMs provide more accurate and culturally appropriate translations than previous machine translation tools. This shift is significant for industries like e-commerce, where localizing content for various regions can directly impact customer engagement and sales.

What are the Challenges?

While LLMs are impressively fluent in generating responses, they can also fabricate information when they lack specific knowledge, presenting fiction as fact. This phenomenon, known as "hallucination," occurs because LLMs don't "understand" information in a human sense—they only produce responses based on the patterns they've identified in their training data. As a result, an LLM might confidently generate an incorrect answer to a factual question. This limitation underscores the importance of context-aware applications like Retrieval-Augmented Generation (RAG) to cross-reference responses with reliable external data sources, which we will discuss later in this chapter.

Moreover, LLMs are trained on massive datasets but are generally not updated after their training phase. This means they can lack awareness of recent events or trends, limiting their relevance in real-time applications. For instance, an LLM trained in 2021 would not be aware of news developments or scientific breakthroughs from 2022 onward. Again, techniques like RAG can be used to supply models with up-to-date information, ensuring that responses remain accurate and current.

As the descendants of Generative AI, LLMs inherit the challenges and considerations. Ethical considerations, especially concerning misinformation, biases, and data privacy. LLMs can inadvertently perpetuate biases in their training data, producing outputs that reflect and even reinforce harmful stereotypes. Moreover, given that LLMs are often trained on publicly available data from the internet, they may unintentionally reproduce personal included in their training set. This can lead to unintended privacy violations, especially if sensitive information resurfaces in generated outputs. Ensuring data privacy while maintaining model effectiveness is an ongoing area of research in AI ethics.

Finally, training LLMs requires enormous computational resources, making it costly and environmentally demanding. Large models consume vast amounts of electricity and data, leading to a high carbon footprint and significant hardware requirements. As such, researchers are exploring ways to make LLMs more efficient in training and deployment by developing smaller, task-specific language models that consume less energy and can be deployed in a broader range of devices.

Multimodal Models: Teaching AI to Think Like Humans

Imagine explaining a complex idea to a friend. You might use words to describe it, gestures to illustrate it, and even pull out your phone to show a picture or video for clarity. Humans are naturally multimodal—we take in the world through sight, sound, and language, combining these inputs to understand and communicate more effectively.

For years, AI systems were confined to one type of data at a time: some worked with text, others with images, and still others with audio. But the rise of multimodal models is changing that, enabling AI to process and generate insights from multiple types of data simultaneously, much like how humans experience the world.

Multimodal models represent a huge leap in AI's evolution. Unlike traditional systems, they break down the walls between data types, allowing AI to draw insights from text, images, videos, and audio at once. Take OpenAI's DALL-E, for instance—a system that turns written descriptions into stunningly detailed images. Or consider Google's MUM (Multitask Unified Model), which can analyze a mix of text, images, and videos to answer complex queries, like helping you plan a hiking trip by comparing routes, gear, and weather forecasts. These models don't just process information—they integrate it, creating a richer, more human-like understanding of the task at hand.

How Does It Work?

At the heart of a multimodal model's power is its ability to understand relationships between different types of data. To do this, it relies on a clever learning process that teaches it to connect dots between modalities—like associating a caption with an image or matching a voice command to an action. Think of it like training a child: you might show them a picture of a cat, say the word "cat," and maybe even let them hear a cat's meow. Over time, they associate the image, sound, and word into a single concept. Multimodal models follow a similar principle.

You shouldn't be surprised that Multimodal models use neural networks to find patterns and connections. During training, they are shown paired examples, such as an image and its description, or a video and the accompanying audio. The model learns to **map relationships** by associating these data types onto a shared representation, essentially creating a universal "language" that connects them.

Advanced multimodal models use **attention mechanisms** to focus on the most relevant parts of each data type. For example, when analyzing an image and a question about it, the model doesn't examine every pixel. It focuses on the parts of the image that are most likely to contain the answer. This allows the system to concentrate on key details and combine them effectively.

Once trained, multimodal models can perform a variety of tasks by combining their understanding of different modalities. For example, they can generate a realistic image based on a text prompt or create a descriptive caption for a video. The output is seamless because the model has learned to think of the modalities as interconnected rather than separate.

Where Can It Apply To?

The power of multimodal models lies in their versatility. Consider healthcare: a doctor might rely on written patient records, X-rays, and recorded symptoms to make a diagnosis. A multimodal AI could combine these inputs into a single, cohesive analysis, spotting patterns a human might miss. In education, a teacher could use an AI system that delivers personalized lessons, blending audio explanations, visual aids, and interactive exercises tailored to a student's needs. And in marketing, brands are using multimodal AI to create advertisements that seamlessly combine catchy slogans with visually striking graphics and perfectly matched soundtracks.

This ability to blend modalities also unlocks creativity in ways we've never seen before. Imagine describing a scene from your favorite novel to an AI and watching it transform your words into a vivid painting, or speaking to your virtual assistant, showing it a picture of your broken appliance, and having it guide you through repairs in real time. Multimodal models turn what was once science fiction into reality, making AI more intuitive and interactive than ever.

What are the Challenges?

While the potential is enormous, building these systems isn't easy. For multimodal models to work, the different types of data, text, images, audio, must align perfectly. A caption for an image or a script for a video needs to match its visual or auditory counterpart exactly, and gathering this kind of synchronized data is a massive challenge. Then there's the issue of scale: training a model to handle just one data type requires vast computational resources, but teaching it to juggle multiple modalities pushes those requirements into the stratosphere. And, as with all advanced AI, the lack of transparency in how these models make decisions can create problems when they're used in sensitive areas like healthcare or hiring.

But the effort is worth it. Multimodal models are more than just a technological milestone. They're reshaping the way we interact with AI and opening the door to a world where machines understand and respond to us more naturally than ever before. By learning to "think" across modalities, these systems bring us closer to an AI that doesn't just process data but experiences it, redefining what's possible in creativity, communication, and collaboration.

Small Language Models (SLMs): Lean, Efficient, and Task-Specific

While Large Language Models (LLMs) like GPT and BERT grab the spotlight in the AI world, their smaller, more agile siblings, Small Language Models (SLMs), are quietly powering a revolution of their own. These lean and efficient models are essential for a wide range of applications, especially when resources are limited or speed is critical. Think of them as specialized experts in the AI world, excelling in specific tasks without the heavy computational demands of their larger counterparts.

How Does It Work?

Imagine taking a master chef's extensive cookbook and distilling it into a set of essential recipes perfectly tailored for everyday cooking. That's essentially what happens with SLMs. They are created by taking the knowledge of a large, powerful language model and compressing it into a smaller, more focused package. This process, often called "knowledge distillation," allows SLMs to retain much of the original model's capabilities while significantly reducing their size and computational needs. This makes them ideal for deployment on devices with limited processing power, like smartphones, smart home devices, or even wearables.

Unlike LLMs trained to be generalists, SLMs are often specialists. They are fine-tuned for specific tasks, such as translating short phrases for one language, generating descriptions for medical products, or answering customer service inquiries for one specific company. This specialization allows them to achieve remarkable efficiency and accuracy without needing vast data or processing power.

Where Can It Apply To?

On-Device AI: SLMs are perfect for powering AI features directly on your smartphone. Think of real-time language translation, voice assistants that respond instantly, or predictive text that seems to know what you want to say before you type it. Thanks to SLMs running efficiently on your device, all of this is possible without the need for constant internet connectivity.

Low-Latency Applications: SLMs excel in situations where speed is paramount. They can provide instant responses in chatbots, real-time translation for live conversations, or even generate closed captions for videos with minimal delay.

Efficient Content Moderation: Social media platforms and online forums can leverage SLMs to quickly and efficiently filter out toxic content, spam, and offensive language, creating a safer and more positive online environment.

Specialized Business Functions: SLMs can be tailored to specific business needs, such as analyzing customer sentiment in financial reports, summarizing legal documents, or even generating personalized marketing materials.

What are the Challenges?

SLMs excel in specific tasks but may struggle with tasks outside their area of expertise. They are not designed to be general-purpose language models like LLMs. Hence, SLMs may not have the same level of nuanced understanding of language as LLMs. They might miss subtle cues or struggle with complex, ambiguous sentences. Also, while SLMs require less training data than LLMs, their smaller datasets can sometimes limit their ability to handle diverse language inputs or unexpected queries.

Knowing where to apply SLMs appropriately may make these challenges less of a problem and more of a feature of SLMs.

Retrieval-Augmented Generation (RAG): Enhancing AI with Real-Time Knowledge

Imagine an AI that can access the entire world's knowledge in real-time, weaving together information from countless sources to provide accurate, up-to-date answers to your questions. This is the promise of Retrieval-Augmented Generation (RAG), a groundbreaking approach to transforming how AI interacts with information.

As Large Language Models (LLMs) push the boundaries of AI's language capabilities, RAG is emerging to solve a persistent issue: keeping AI responses accurate, relevant, and current. RAG combines generative AI models with powerful retrieval techniques to provide contextually relevant answers grounded in external knowledge bases. This approach addresses two significant challenges of LLMs we saw earlier: outdated training data and the tendency to "hallucinate." RAG is transforming generative AI into a more reliable, trustworthy tool across industries by allowing LLMs to access real-time, factual information.

How Does It Work?

Think of RAG as a librarian and a storyteller working together. The librarian (the retrieval component) finds the most relevant books and articles based on your question. Then, the storyteller (the generative AI model) uses those resources to craft a compelling and informative answer. RAG pairs a generative AI model, like an LLM, with a retrieval component that actively searches for relevant information in real-time.

When a user asks a question, the RAG model analyzes the query and retrieves pertinent information from an external database or knowledge source. This could be a document database, a proprietary knowledge base, or even recent internet sources. **Query Analysis and Retrieval** help identify relevant facts, statistics, or documents based on the context of the question.

Once the retrieval component has gathered relevant information, the generative AI model steps in for **Response Generation**. Rather than creating a response purely from its training data, the model incorporates the retrieved facts to generate a grounded, contextually accurate answer. This blending of information allows the AI to provide coherent answers based on verified, up-to-date sources.

RAG systems can also incorporate **Feedback Loop for Improvement** to learn and improve over time. For example, suppose a user corrects an AI response. In that case, this correction can refine future answers, helping the model become more accurate and reliable as it learns from interactions.

By combining retrieval and generation, RAG offers the best of both worlds: the fluency and coherence of a generative model with the factual grounding of a retrieval system. This method is particularly valuable for applications where accuracy is essential, such as customer support, research assistance, and legal or medical information retrieval.

Where Can It Apply To?

Customer Support and FAQ Handling: RAG models excel in customer support scenarios where users need accurate information pulled from a company's database, such as policies, manuals, or product specifications. Imagine contacting customer support and receiving an instant, accurate answer to your question, even about a highly specific product detail or a recent company policy change. RAG makes this possible by giving AI access to the latest company information. This helps companies provide fast, reliable support while alleviating the burden on human agents.

Research Assistance: Up-to-date information is essential in fields like academic research, finance, and healthcare. RAG allows AI models to search the latest studies, financial reports, or health guidelines before generating responses, ensuring that the most current data informs answers. Instead of sifting through mountains of scientific papers, a researcher could use RAG-powered AI to quickly identify the most relevant studies and summarize their key findings.

Legal and Regulatory Guidance: Legal professionals often rely on detailed information from case law, statutes, and regulatory documents. RAG can help lawyers or regulatory experts by pulling directly from these resources and providing reliable, source-backed answers that comply with current regulations. Using RAG, a lawyer could instantly access relevant case law and statutes, ensuring their legal advice is always up-to-date and accurate.

Educational Tools and Personalized Learning: RAG enables the creation of more robust educational tools that pull from up-to-date educational content, academic sources, or multimedia databases. This ensures that students and educators receive accurate, diverse information tailored to individual learning needs, making educational content more engaging and relevant.

What are the Challenges?

The quality of an RAG model's answers depends heavily on the quality and relevance of the data in the external knowledge base. If the retrieval source contains outdated, biased, or incomplete information, the AI's responses may reflect those flaws. This reliance underscores the importance of maintaining accurate, diverse, and well-curated retrieval sources.

Retrieval steps add extra processing time to each response, which can slightly increase latency. For high-speed applications, this additional time could impact the user experience. Techniques like caching commonly requested data or improving retrieval algorithms can help mitigate these delays, but careful optimization is needed to maintain efficiency.

Privacy and security become crucial if an RAG model retrieves information from sensitive databases or real-time internet sources. Ensuring that retrieval sources are secure, anonymized, and compliant with privacy regulations is vital, especially in the healthcare or finance sectors, where data sensitivity is high. Even with RAG, the reasoning behind an AI's answer might not always be transparent.

While we need to be aware of these potential issues, RAG sets the stage for a new generation of intelligent systems that simulate understanding and genuinely reflect the most current and reliable knowledge available.

Explainable AI (XAI): Building Trust Through Transparency

In a world increasingly reliant on AI, it's no longer enough for these intelligent systems to simply provide answers. We need to understand *how* they arrive at those answers. Explainable AI (XAI) is leading the charge in demystifying AI's decision-making processes, bringing transparency and accountability to this powerful technology. XAI is like shining a light into the "black box" of AI, allowing us to see the inner workings and understand the reasoning behind its predictions and recommendations.

Imagine applying for a loan, and an AI system denies your application. Wouldn't you want to know why? XAI aims to provide those answers. It involves a set of techniques and practices designed to clarify the decision-making processes of complex AI models, especially those that tend to function as "black boxes," like deep neural networks. XAI seeks to open this black box, providing insights into which features influenced a decision and how the model arrived at its conclusions.

How Does It Work?

Post-Hoc Explanations are techniques applied after a model has made a decision, allowing users to interpret and analyze the factors influencing a specific output. Think of it like a detective retracing the steps of a crime to understand how it happened. Examples include LIME (Local Interpretable Model-agnostic Explanations) and SHAP (SHapley Additive exPlanations), which work by approximating complex models with simpler, interpretable models for individual predictions. For instance, if an AI model rejects a loan application, SHAP can highlight factors—such as income level or credit history—that contributed most to this decision.

On the other hand, instead of explaining a model after the fact, **Intrinsic Interpretability** focuses on designing inherently understandable models. These models are like clear glass boxes, where you can see the entire process unfold. Decision trees and linear regression are examples of intrinsically interpretable models because their structures clearly show how input features lead to specific outcomes. Although these models may not perform as well as complex neural networks for some tasks, they provide clarity in fields where transparency is non-negotiable.

Where Can It Apply To?

Healthcare and Medical Diagnosis: XAI can help doctors understand why an AI model recommends a particular treatment plan, ensuring that medical decisions are made clearly and confidently.

Financial Services and Credit Scoring: XAI can provide transparency in loan applications and credit scoring, helping individuals understand the factors influencing their financial assessments.

Legal and Regulatory Compliance: XAI can help ensure that AI systems used in the legal domain are fair, unbiased, and compliant with regulations.

Autonomous Vehicles: XAI can help explain the decisions made by self-driving cars, building trust and understanding in this emerging technology.

What are the Challenges?

Some XAI techniques provide approximate interpretations of complex models, meaning their explanations may not perfectly represent the AI's actual workings but are just approximations. Sometimes, easier-to-explain models might not be as accurate as more complex, "black box" models, which results in a trade-off with model performance. Moreover, providing detailed explanations for very large AI models can be computationally expensive and challenging to scale.

Despite these limitations, we should know that as AI becomes more prominent in our lives, it's crucial to ensure that these systems are transparent, accountable, and fair. Hence, XAI is essential for preventing bias, discrimination, and misuse of AI. It also plays a vital role in complying with emerging AI regulations, such as the EU's GDPR, which grants individuals the "right to explanation" for automated decisions that affect them. XAI pushes the boundaries not just a solution for technical issues; it's also an ethical one.

Federated Learning: Privacy-Preserving AI for a Connected World

Imagine a world where AI can learn from the collective wisdom of millions of devices without ever accessing your personal data. This is the vision of Federated Learning (FL), a revolutionary approach to AI training redefining privacy and collaboration. In an era where data privacy is paramount, Federated Learning offers a groundbreaking approach to AI training by allowing models to learn from decentralized data sources without ever collecting the data itself.

Unlike traditional Machine Learning, where data is aggregated on a central server, federated learning enables data to remain on the device, with only model updates being shared. This setup is invaluable for healthcare, finance, and telecommunications industries, where data sensitivity and privacy are non-negotiable. By distributing learning across devices while maintaining data privacy, federated learning brings both security and intelligence to AI applications in our increasingly connected world.

How Does It Work?

Think of Federated Learning as a team of scientists working on a cure for a disease. Each scientist conducts experiments in their own lab, using their own unique data and equipment. They then share their findings with each other, combining their knowledge to develop a more effective treatment. However, they never share their actual patient data, only the insights they've gained from it. This is similar to how Federated Learning works. It distributes the learning process across multiple devices, such as smartphones or edge devices, allowing each to contribute to model training without sharing raw data.

The first step to make it work is to initialize a global model on a central server and distribute it to participating devices, including users' smartphones, IoT devices, or local servers in organizations. This model is a blank slate that will be trained based on insights from each device's local data.

Each device trains the model locally using its own data, creating model updates that reflect the patterns or insights derived from the device's specific data. For example, a smartphone might train a predictive text model based on the user's typing habits, or a hospital server might train a medical model based on patient data.

Once each device has completed its local training, only the updated model parameters (not the raw data) are returned to the central server. These updates are aggregated to refine the global model. This aggregation process typically involves averaging the parameters across devices, creating a shared model that reflects learning from the entire network without exposing individual data.

The updated global model is then sent back to the devices, and the process repeats iteratively until the model reaches a satisfactory performance level. This iterative process enables federated learning to continually improve the model while ensuring that sensitive data remains on each device, protected from centralization risks.

Where Can It Apply To?

Healthcare and Medical Research: In healthcare, federated learning allows hospitals and research institutions to collectively train models on patient data without ever sharing that data across institutions. Imagine hospitals worldwide collaborating to develop a more accurate model for diagnosing rare diseases, all while keeping each patient's data secure and confidential within their own hospital's system. Federated learning makes this possible. This is crucial for developing predictive models in areas like disease detection and treatment recommendation, where access to diverse datasets is necessary, but data privacy must be preserved. For example, federated learning could enable hospitals to create a shared diagnostic model for identifying rare diseases, drawing from diverse patient data without risking privacy breaches.

Mobile and Personalized Applications: On-device AI applications, such as predictive text, personalized recommendations, and voice recognition, often rely on highly individualized data. Federated learning enables these apps to learn from each user's preferences while keeping personal data on the device, thus enhancing the personalization of AI-powered experiences without compromising privacy. Your smartphone can learn to predict your next word or suggest relevant emojis based on your unique typing style without ever sending your personal data to the cloud. Google, for example, uses federated learning in its Google keyboard app to improve predictive text and autocorrect suggestions based on user-specific typing patterns.

Financial Services: Banks and financial institutions can use federated learning to collaboratively develop models for credit scoring, fraud detection, and risk assessment without sharing sensitive client information. Banks can work together to detect fraudulent transactions more effectively by training a shared AI model on their combined data without ever exchanging sensitive customer information. Federated learning enables this secure collaboration. By training these models on decentralized data from multiple institutions, federated learning enhances model accuracy and robustness without requiring raw financial data to leave individual organizations. This approach is particularly valuable in ensuring compliance with strict financial regulations around data sharing and privacy.

Smart Homes and IoT: Federated learning is also advancing the field of smart homes and IoT, where connected devices gather vast amounts of personal data. From smart thermostats to wearable health devices, federated learning enables these devices to learn from user data locally, updating models to become smarter and more responsive without centralizing data. This privacy-focused approach helps make IoT devices more reliable and user-friendly while maintaining the security of personal information.

What are the Challenges?

Coordinating updates across an extensive network of devices can result in high communication overhead, as each device must send its model parameters back to the central server. This back-and-forth exchange can introduce latency, especially when updates are frequent or devices have limited connectivity, such as in remote areas. Optimization techniques are needed to streamline communication and manage bandwidth demands.

Moreover, in federated learning, each participating device may have different processing power, memory, and connectivity, leading to variability in model updates. This device heterogeneity can affect model convergence, as some devices may produce more robust updates than others. Balancing the contributions of diverse devices is a technical challenge in federated learning.

While federated learning improves privacy, it doesn't guarantee data quality, as each device may have unique biases or data inconsistencies. Additionally, federated learning is susceptible to security risks such as model poisoning attacks, where compromised devices send manipulated updates. Advanced aggregation techniques and security protocols are being developed to mitigate these risks and improve model integrity.

Those are the challenges, but Federated Learning will still play a central role in shaping the future of AI as privacy concerns and regulatory requirements continue to grow. This paradigm shift can unlock new levels of collaboration and innovation, paving the way for a more inclusive, secure, and democratic future for AI.

Human-Centered AI: Empowering Users Through Collaboration and Control

Imagine AI as a partner, not just a tool—a partner that understands our needs, learns from our expertise, and collaborates with us to achieve our goals. This is the essence of Human-Centered AI (HCAI), a philosophy that places human values, insights, and oversight at the forefront of AI development. HCAI recognizes that AI is most effective when it works in harmony with human intelligence, augmenting our abilities rather than replacing them. This approach is particularly crucial in healthcare, finance, and business intelligence, where human expertise and context are essential for making informed decisions.

How Does It Work?

In 2020, I published a whitepaper, "Human-Centered AI for BI Industry," with other industry leaders under Linux Foundation LF AI & Data. One of the key concepts I presented in the publication is that in order to build trust, we need to keep improving AI through iterative learning and constant monitoring, a process I call "machine teaching."

Rather than setting an AI loose and letting it work without oversight, we should guide it, review its outputs, and refine it over time. AI is not static—it can and should be continually improved through feedback and oversight, much like a student who learns and grows with guidance. With each iteration, AI systems can be fine-tuned to meet the specific needs and ethical standards of the environments in which they operate.

Since humans are involved in teaching the machine, this improves transparency and makes the final result more interpretable. We are part of it to correct it if the result doesn't make sense. This user-controlled and feedback-driven approach can guide and influence AI, providing feedback and correcting its mistakes. AI will then learn and evolve based on human input, creating a dynamic partnership where humans and machines learn from each other.

Where Can It Apply To?

Short answer: Everywhere AI is used! However, there are two areas specifically applicable to incorporate with HCAI. The first area is Data Input and Annotation. Instead of manually labeling every single data point, humans can provide initial guidance and then step in to clarify ambiguous cases or correct errors. This makes the data labeling process more efficient and accurate, while also allowing AI to learn from human expertise. This is particularly useful in BI contexts where AI might struggle to identify anomalies or patterns in complex data. AI can learn and improve its understanding by flagging uncertain cases and prompting the user for clarification.

In addition, we can adjust the model dynamically by providing feedback after an AI model is deployed. When AI is unsure about a prediction or recommendation, it can flag it for human review. Humans can then accept, reject, or modify the AI's output, providing valuable feedback that allows the AI to learn and adapt. This dynamic feedback loop is essential for building AI systems that are responsive, reliable, and aligned with human values.

What are the Challenges?

The human feedback loop is a cornerstone of HCAI, enabling systems to learn and adapt continuously. However, this reliance on human input also introduces the risk of embedding human biases into the system. If users unintentionally inject their personal, cultural, or systemic biases into feedback, the AI may adopt and amplify those biases over time.

Consider hiring platforms that use HCAI to evaluate resumes. If hiring managers favor certain demographic groups or educational backgrounds, their feedback could teach the system to replicate those preferences, leading to discriminatory outcomes. Similarly, in criminal justice applications, biases in historical data or judgments can perpetuate unfair treatment of marginalized groups, even when a human-in-the-loop system is designed to provide oversight. The iterative nature of feedback loops means that small biases can snowball into significant problems, especially if they are not detected and corrected early. Left unchecked, this creates a cycle where AI systems perpetuate inequities rather than mitigate them.

HCAI systems also require significant resources to build and maintain. Unlike fully automated systems operating independently after deployment, HCAI demands ongoing human participation at multiple stages. Data labeling, feedback collection, interface design, and retraining processes all require continuous effort from teams of experts and users. This commitment can translate to feedback fatigue, which users may ask, "Should AI help me by taking away my workload? Why do I get more work now to help it?"

These challenges are real. However, having HCAI brings us one step closer to the true integration of AI in our lives, which benefits us because we are no longer just bystanders. By reducing biases through audits and diverse input and removing feedback fatigue through efficient response mechanisms, we can build systems that empower users and adapt to their needs. HCAI transforms AI into a partner, not just a tool, creating a future where humans and machines collaborate meaningfully and ethically.

CHAPTER 9

Happily Ever After – The Convergence of AI with Other Modernized Technologies

Let's imagine AI can solve problems that are currently impossible, create unbreakable security systems, and transport us to fantastical virtual worlds. This is the promise of AI convergence, where Artificial Intelligence joins forces with other cutting-edge technologies to unlock new levels of innovation and possibility.

As Artificial Intelligence continues to evolve, it's finding powerful allies in a range of emerging technologies. This convergence of AI with fields like Quantum Computing, Blockchain, and Extended Reality (AR & VR) signals a new era of possibilities, where each technology enhances the others' capabilities to address complex challenges and unlock new potential. This convergence is not just about adding capabilities; it's about creating synergies where the whole is greater than the sum of its parts.

AI's ability to learn and adapt, combined with the unique strengths of quantum computing, blockchain, and extended reality, is leading to previously unimaginable breakthroughs. In this chapter, we explore how Quantum Computing, Blockchain, and Extended Reality combine with AI to inspire new applications, broaden horizons, and demonstrate the extraordinary power of collaborative innovation.

And there is one bonus I guarantee you cannot find anywhere else yet. Let's roll!

Quantum Computing and AI: Accelerating Intelligence

How can you find a book in a library the size of the universe? Classical computers would painstakingly check one book at a time, but a quantum computer could, in theory, open every book simultaneously. This is the essence of quantum computing—a revolutionary approach that leverages the principles of quantum mechanics to process information in ways that classical computers simply cannot.

At the heart of quantum computing are quantum bits, or qubits (I know it's close. But no, not Cupid, it's qubits! ☺). Unlike traditional bits that exist in a state of either 0 or 1, qubits can exist in multiple states at once thanks to a phenomenon called superposition. This means a qubit can be both 0 and 1 simultaneously, allowing quantum computers to handle a massive number of calculations simultaneously. Another quantum property, entanglement, enables entangled qubits to be instantly correlated with each other, no matter the distance separating them. These properties allow quantum computers to solve complex problems exponentially faster than their classical counterparts.

So, how does this relate to Artificial Intelligence? AI, especially machine learning and neural networks, requires immense computational power to process large datasets and perform complex calculations. Traditional computers, even the most powerful supercomputers, face limitations in speed and capacity when tackling these tasks. Quantum computing offers a way to break through these barriers by providing the computational horsepower needed to accelerate AI algorithms beyond current capabilities.

Think of AI as a race car and quantum computing as a rocket engine. The race car is already fast and efficient on the track (our current computational landscape). However, attaching a rocket engine propels it into an entirely new realm of speed and performance. By integrating quantum computing with AI, we're not just making incremental improvements but redefining what's possible.

A compelling example of this synergy is in drug discovery. Developing a new medication involves analyzing countless molecular combinations to identify candidates that might effectively treat a disease. Classical computers struggle with this task due to the astronomical number of possible interactions of molecules. Quantum computing can easily handle these calculations, allowing AI algorithms to simulate and evaluate molecular structures and interactions at unprecedented speeds. This could dramatically reduce the time and cost required to bring new, life-saving drugs to market.

By merging the adaptive learning capabilities of AI with the computational might of quantum computers, we're poised to tackle problems previously deemed unsolvable. This powerful combination could lead to breakthroughs in cryptography, optimization problems, financial modeling, and more. The convergence of quantum computing and AI doesn't just enhance what each can do individually; it creates a synergistic effect that accelerates innovation and opens doors to new possibilities we are only beginning to imagine.

Blockchain and AI: Harmonizing Intelligence and Trust

What if we are in a world where every handshake agreement is instantly notarized, transparent to all parties, and immutable for eternity? This is the promise of blockchain—a revolutionary technology that creates a secure and decentralized ledger of transactions. At its core, blockchain is a chain of blocks containing data, each linked to the previous one using cryptographic principles. This design ensures that once information is added, it cannot be altered or deleted without consensus from the entire network, making it exceptionally secure and trustworthy.

Blockchain operates on a decentralized network of computers, or nodes, each holding a copy of the entire ledger. When a transaction occurs, it is validated by these nodes through a consensus mechanism before being added to a block. This process eliminates the need for a central authority, like a bank or government, to verify transactions. It's like having a public bulletin board where every entry is time-stamped and locked behind a glass case—visible to all but unchangeable.

Now, think of Artificial Intelligence as the Yin—dynamic, adaptive, and probabilistic. AI models evolve and learn from data, constantly updating their understanding of patterns and making predictions. Blockchain, on the other hand, is the Yang—static, secure, and deterministic. It provides a permanent record that doesn't change once it is written. While AI thrives on flexibility and learning, blockchain offers stability and trust. Together, they form a harmonious balance, complementing each other's strengths.

Consider a flowing river (AI) and a sturdy bridge (Blockchain). The river represents AI's ever-changing, learning nature, continuously moving and adapting to the landscape. The bridge symbolizes blockchain's solidity and permanence, providing a reliable structure over which the dynamic river of data can flow safely. By combining the two, we create a system in which the unwavering trustworthiness of blockchain underpins AI's constant evolution.

Applying this concept to a smart healthcare system, AI algorithms require access to vast amounts of sensitive patient data—such as medical histories, test results, and treatment outcomes—to analyze and provide personalized treatment plans. However, sharing this sensitive information raises significant privacy and security concerns.

By integrating blockchain technology, each patient's data is securely managed through a combination of off-chain storage and blockchain-based access controls. The actual patient data is stored securely off-chain in encrypted databases. The blockchain records encrypted references or cryptographic hashes of this data, serving as a tamper-proof ledger that ensures data integrity. Patients control who can access their data through permissions managed by smart contracts on the blockchain. Only authorized AI models and healthcare providers, who have the necessary decryption keys and permissions, can access the data they need. This setup ensures data privacy and integrity while allowing AI to process the information essential for personalized care.

For instance, during a global pandemic, rapid analysis of patient data is crucial for identifying patterns and developing effective treatments. AI can swiftly analyze anonymized and encrypted data from millions of patients to predict disease spread and suggest interventions. Blockchain ensures that this sensitive data is securely shared among trusted parties without the risk of tampering or unauthorized access. By utilizing a permissioned blockchain network, only authorized healthcare organizations and researchers can participate, adhering to strict data protection regulations. Patients know their data is securely managed, with all access and usage transparently recorded on the blockchain, and only used with their consent as governed by smart contracts. This combination of AI and blockchain accelerates medical research and improves patient outcomes while upholding the highest privacy and security standards.

By merging AI's intelligence with blockchain's trustworthiness, we unlock new possibilities across various industries. In finance, AI can detect fraudulent activities in real time, while blockchain securely records all transactions, making audits straightforward and transparent. In supply chain management, AI optimizes logistics, and blockchain provides an immutable record of a product's journey from manufacturer to consumer, enhancing transparency and trust.

In essence, the convergence of AI and blockchain is like the Yin and Yang of modern technology—balancing adaptability with reliability. AI brings the power to learn and predict, while blockchain offers a foundation of trust and security. Together, they create systems that are not only smart but also resilient and trustworthy, paving the way for innovations that can profoundly transform how we interact with the digital world.

Extended Reality and AI: Merging Realities with Intelligence

With the promise of Extended Reality (XR), an umbrella term that encompasses Virtual Reality (VR), Augmented Reality (AR), and Mixed Reality (MR), we are entering a world where the boundaries between the physical and digital realms dissolve—a place where you can walk through ancient cities, interact with virtual characters, or have real-time information seamlessly overlaid onto your surroundings. XR technologies aim to enhance or transform our perception of the world by immersing us in virtual environments (VR), overlaying digital information onto the real world (AR), or blending both to create interactive experiences where physical and digital objects coexist and interact (MR).

At its core, XR uses devices like headsets, glasses, or smartphones to present digital content that aligns with our physical environment. VR creates a fully immersive digital experience, isolating users from the real world. AR overlays digital elements onto the real world, enhancing what we see, hear, and feel. MR goes a step further by allowing digital and physical objects to interact in real-time, creating experiences where the virtual and real are nearly indistinguishable.

When injected with AI, it brings intelligence and adaptability to XR environments, making them more responsive, personalized, and interactive. While XR provides the canvas for immersive experiences, AI acts as the artist who paints a dynamic and evolving picture based on user interactions. Together, they create a synergy that elevates user experiences to new heights.

Think of XR as a sophisticated stage and AI as an orchestra conductor. The stage is set with all the props and lighting (the XR environment), but without the conductor (AI), the performance lacks harmony and responsiveness. The conductor interprets the mood, directs the musicians (digital elements), and adapts the performance in real-time to captivate the audience. Similarly, AI infuses XR environments with the ability to understand and react to users, creating a harmonious and engaging experience.

Instead of walking into a traditional brick-and-mortar store, what if you enter a clothing store where you put on AR glasses? As you browse, AI analyzes your style preferences, body measurements, and even your mood. It then overlays virtual clothing onto your reflection in a mirror, showing you exactly how different outfits would look without the need to try them on physically. If you express interest in a particular item, AI can suggest complementary accessories or alternative styles, all in real-time. This not only enhances the shopping experience but also provides retailers with valuable insights into customer preferences.

In another scenario, consider remote collaboration in a professional setting. With AI-powered MR headsets, team members worldwide can appear as holographic projections in a shared virtual workspace. AI facilitates natural language processing for seamless communication, translates languages in real-time, and even reads facial expressions to gauge emotional cues. This creates an environment where distance is irrelevant, and collaboration is as intuitive as if everyone were in the same room.

By merging XR's ability to create immersive environments with AI's capacity for learning and adaptation, we unlock experiences that are not only visually impressive but also deeply interactive and personalized. In education, students can explore complex scientific concepts through interactive simulations that adapt to their learning pace. In healthcare, surgeons can practice intricate procedures in a virtual environment that responds to their actions, improving their skills without risking patients.

The convergence of Extended Reality and Artificial Intelligence is more than just a technological advancement; it's a transformative leap that redefines how we interact with digital content. XR provides the platform for new realities, while AI brings these realities to life with intelligence and adaptability. Together, they offer unprecedented opportunities to enrich our personal and professional lives, making experiences more engaging, informative, and tailored to our individual needs.

Bonus: Federaiota

What are you talking about? Federaitoa? No worries; I expect you will react this way when I share this term with you.

In early 2024, Dr. Wil Ngwa invited me to address an AI keynote at the Global Health Catalyst Summit. In our conversation, he challenged me to think BIG: "If the sky is the limit and budget is not a problem, what can we do for healthcare?"

The challenge was accepted, and the summit's theme was Cancer Moonshot 2.0. What is something bigger than that? Well, cancer is a problem, but it's only a subset of the whole healthcare system. Moon is hard to go, but SpaceX has already had a mission to Mars. What if we aim, not a Cancer Moonshot, but a "**Healthcare Marsshot**"?

As you may know, our current healthcare system has some room for improvement. Even though AI is pretty powerful today, it still has limitations. Well, there are at least four I can think of.

First of all, it is data privacy. Traditional AI requires all data to be collected and stored in a centralized location before a Machine Learning algorithm can learn from it and train the model. This immediately breaches data privacy because data is collected.

Secondly, data is fire. Let's imagine I have a torch. I passed the fire on my torch to yours. When I walk away from you, you can continuously pass my fire to someone else without my knowledge and permission. Data behaves the same. If I give you my data to train your AI model, I lose control of my data. You can keep sharing it without my knowledge and my approval. That's why the value of the data depreciates immediately the moment it is shared by someone else, unlike tangible objects, which will still depreciate but at a much slower rate.

Third, ChatGPT and Gemini are very powerful Large Language Models (LLMs), and they train the model based on publicly available data. However, a lot more data are not publicly available but proprietary, especially sensitive data such as healthcare records. If our current AI is already so powerful without that, the potential of incorporating proprietary data in AI is unimaginable.

Fourth and finally, the AI model is great and useful. But how can we connect it to the real-time conditions so that it can provide real-time advice when we need it?

Those shortcomings make me think for months about how to improve the current AI implementation to something even better in healthcare. What if we can enhance traditional AI by privacy-preserving federated learning with decentralized real-time data via IoT? What if we can build a platform **connecting** all patients, doctors, researchers, and all kinds of healthcare organizations together to enable data sharing and ML model training **privately**? The trained model (a traditional AI model or LLM by GenAI) will then be deployed to users so that they can get **personalized** advice **proactively** when needed.

What a mouthful! But that's the Marsshot we are talking about: combining the power of Federated Learning, AI, IoT, and Data. I first shared this concept publicly in June 2024 at the Global Health Summit in Washington, D.C., and it was well received. When can we fully accomplish this Healthcare Marsshot mission? I don't have the exact day, but we are working towards it to bring the finish line closer and closer.

Like a marriage in real life, the convergence of AI with other modernized technologies—whether it's Quantum Computing, Blockchain, or Extended Reality, Federaiota—requires more than just initial excitement. Achieving "happily ever after" is a continuous process of understanding, adjustment, and compromise. AI must learn to adapt to the unique strengths and limitations of each technology it partners with, while these technologies, in turn, evolve to integrate AI's capabilities seamlessly. This partnership isn't always perfect or straightforward, but with collaboration and shared goals, the potential is limitless. Together, these technologies can create a future that's not just innovative but deeply transformative, reminding us that true success comes from working in harmony toward a common vision.

CONCLUSION

So What?!

After traversing the intricate landscapes of Artificial Intelligence throughout this book, a pressing question remains: **So what?** What does all this mean for you, our children, and our society?

Allow me to recount a conversation with my son in Chapter 1 that encapsulates the essence of this question. One day, he asked me, "If I use it to do my homework and my teacher cannot tell it's not me doing that, then that is AI?" Before the rise of tools like ChatGPT, my response was rooted in the marvel of possibility: "As a second grader, I'd be super impressed if you could develop an AI model to do your homework. But I'd be equally proud if you found a way to use a model developed by someone else to help with your homework."

Today, with AI models readily accessible, using AI to assist with homework has become second nature for many kids (though many schools ban the use of it). This shift necessitates my updated response. AI can streamline tasks that once took hours or days, but how you use this power defines its impact on you.

A layperson might accept whatever AI outputs without question, presenting it as their own work. This passive approach can lead to mediocrity, as they become controlled by technology, relinquishing their critical thinking. In contrast, a smart individual uses AI as a starting point—an assistant that provides raw material to analyze, organize, and optimize before crafting the final solution. This active engagement not only enhances the quality of the work but also hones one's skills, making the person smarter through proper utilization of technology. This is also my stand when I tell my son about using AI in his study.

Those saying "Using AI to get an answer is cheating" are like people 25 years ago who said, "Using Google for research is cheating" because you should go to the library and flip through books and newspapers to do your research. The real question is, "Are you using Google results as is without even thinking if the result makes sense?" If yes, then you are not just cheating; you are dump-copying. After you get your Google result, you still need to use your critical thinking to distill the material and decide what information is true and which is fake, right?

This brings up a question in many minds: "Will AI take away my job?" The answer isn't a simple yes or no. **Yes**, if you allow technology to control you and replace your unique human contributions. **No**, if you take control of it, integrating AI as a tool that enhances your capabilities.

Think back to 1885 when Karl Benz invented the first automobile. There was likely a jockey who asked, "Will this machine take away my job?" In a sense, it did change the transportation landscape, but it also opened up new avenues. Today, there are far more drivers than there ever were horse riders, in terms of both numbers and percentage, and entirely new industries have emerged around automobiles.

Talking about cars, consider Tesla and Uber—both are in the transportation industry, but their approaches are very different. Tesla reinvented the car itself, pioneering electric vehicles and autonomous driving technologies. They focused on inventing new ways for cars to work. On the other hand, Uber utilized existing technologies like GPS and mobile apps to revolutionize transportation services. They didn't invent the car but transformed how we use it.

In the realm of AI, some people invent new algorithms and models, pushing the boundaries of what's possible. Others apply these trained models to create innovative solutions that benefit communities. Neither path is inherently better; they represent different ways of engaging with and advancing technology.

When contemplating AI, shifting the focus from the technology to the problem at hand is essential. Allow me to borrow the most crucial lesson I learned from the I-CORPS program I went through as a result of the SBIR Award we received from the National Institutes of Health (NIH): *It is not because someone wants a drill; they just need a hole.* The drill is merely a means to an end. Similarly, AI is a tool to solve problems and achieve goals that matter to us. Therefore, I shared this earlier in my X (formerly known as Twitter):

Technology is just a toy for a geek, if it doesn't provide value to the user.

By centering our attention on the challenges we want to address—be it healthcare, education, environmental conservation, or any other field—we can harness AI effectively without getting lost in the complexities of the technology itself.

AI is booming, but it's still in its infancy. True maturation will occur when we no longer talk about AI as something special or separate but when it's seamlessly integrated into the fabric of our lives. Remember about 30 years ago when companies boasted about having internet connectivity? Today, such a statement would draw puzzled looks because the internet has become a ubiquitous part of our daily existence. We no longer marvel at it; we use it.

The same will happen with AI. As it becomes more ingrained in our tools, services, and experiences, we will stop referring to it explicitly. Instead, we will focus on what we're achieving with it—the diseases we're curing, the knowledge we're uncovering, and the connections we're fostering. The moment we take it for granted is the moment this technology becomes truly mature.

AI is not a distant, abstract concept confined to laboratories and tech giants. It's a dynamic force reshaping industries, education, and personal lives. But like any tool, its value depends on how we wield it.

This book is in no way making you an AI expert. But I hope I have done my job to Plainify AI enough to boost your AI journey. The fact that you read until this very last sentence has already made you one step ahead of many others. But don't stop here, as the game has just begun!

Acknowledgments

If I tell you that this book results from a blindfolded monkey that keeps hitting the keyboard randomly for months, I bet you think I am crazy. Compared to what is shared in this book, the underlying principles guiding the operation of this world are way more sophisticated. Hence, if there is no way all letters, words, and punctuation come together by chance to form this book, there must be a more intelligent creator designing this universe, not by artificial intelligence but as the source of intelligence. It is Him who provides me with all I need to finish this book. It is Him who loves me and dies for me on the cross. Thank you, my savior, Lord Jesus!

Fifty years ago, He gave me my parents, who gave birth and nurtured me so I could learn different knowledge to become who I am today. Thank you, my parents.

He also gave me my children. Talking to them inspired me to many ideas in this book. Observing and teaching them helps me to reflect on myself. Thank you, my kids.

My kids would not be in this order today without my in-laws' tendered hearts and taking good care of their even very minor details in different areas. Thank you, my in-laws.

Last, I would not have my in-laws or kids without this person. She took care of everything at home while I wrote this book, worked on my business, and traveled to different parts of the world to share my vision. Nothing could have become a reality without her sacrifice. She sharpened me to be a better person, though sometimes it's painful, to be honest. She is a precious gift God has given me. Thank you, my wife.

www.ingramcontent.com/pod-product-compliance
Lightning Source LLC
Chambersburg PA
CBHW071131050326

40690CB00008B/1417